McDONNELL-DOUGLAS F-15 EAGLE

A PHOTO CHRONICLE

Bill Holder & Mike Wallace

Foreword by General John M. Loh
Commander, Air Combat Command

Schiffer Military/Aviation History
Atglen, PA

Acknowledgements
Patrick Louden, Public Affairs, Pratt & Whitney
Public Affairs Officers at many F-15 operational units
Lee Whitney, Public Affairs Office, McDonnell-Douglas Corporation
Paul Guse, Public Affairs Office, McDonnell-Douglas Corporation
Captain Tracy O'Grady-Walsh, ASC Public Affairs Office
Diana Cornelisse, ASC History Office
David Menard, Air Force Museum Research Department
Cliff Bushey, Marketing Communications, Martin-Marietta.
Spencer P. Lane, Amos Newspapers
Captain Larry Blaker, ASC Public Affairs Office

Book Design by Robert Biondi.

Library of Congress Catalog Number: 94-66965

Printed in China.
ISBN: 0-88740-662-9

We are interested in hearing from authors with book ideas on related topics.

Published by Schiffer Publishing Ltd.
77 Lower Valley Road
Atglen, PA 19310
Please write for a free catalog.
This book may be purchased from the publisher.
Please include $2.95 postage.
Try your bookstore first.

CONTENTS

MIKE LOH

FOREWORD

When the first Eagle rolled out in June of 1972, it opened up a new era for the U.S. Air Force. The design of the F-15 represented a fundamental shift in U.S. air planning – a shift from multi-purpose aircraft to those with uncompromised design features for a specific mission. The F-15 was the first pure air superiority fighter developed by the USAF since the F-86 Sabre in 1948. Since the Sabre, all of our fighters had been either "fighter-bombers" like the F-100 Super Sabre, F-105 Thunderchief, and the F-4 Phantom, or "pure" interceptors like the F-102 Delta Dagger and the F-106 Delta Dart.

As the Eagle went through its paces, it proved to be every bit the air superiority fighter we had hoped for. It could accelerate while climbing vertically, and despite its size, it could turn much tighter than the F-4 Phantom or any other existing fighter. But, like the bird it was named for, the Eagle's eyes gives it its most decisive advantage. With an effective radar range off more than 100 miles, it could "see before being seen," allowing it to strike an unsuspecting foe at the time and place of the pilot's choosing.

One of the key lessons learned very early in Vietn... the importance of quickly winning "tota... MiG-17s, and MiG-19s ... 15 ... wou...

roll... ma... im... ag... d... s... p... t...

of their Air Force we permanently blinded them. Without an effective intelligence network the stage was set for a secret move of two full corps, with over 200,000 troops, more than 250 miles. It resulted in the most successful use of the flanking maneuver in modern warfare and its success was totally dependant on the element of surprise and unrestricted freedom of movement across the battlefield. Air supremacy made this possible. Throughout the conflict, flying Combat Air Patrol guaranteed that Coalition land, sea and air forces could maneuver, deploy, resupply, stockpile, and fight as we desired. They provided a textbook example of what air supremacy means for both the country who has it, and the one that does not.

By the end of the Persian Gulf conflict, our Eagles had flown more than 5,900 sorties and been credited with 33 of the U.S.'s 38 air-to-air victories.

Over the years the F-15 force has undergone several upgrades. These changes ensure it remains the world's foremost air superiority fighter. While almost identical in appearance to its older brother the F-15 A/B, the the F-15 C/D received an extensive avionics upgrade, carries nearly 1,900 lbs. more internal fuel, and can add 10,000 lbs. more external fuel when configured with conformal ...tanks. The versatility of the F-15 design was ... demonstrated by the development of the F-... two-seat version of the Eagle optimized for ...ange, adverse weather, precision surface at-

...ur allies also recognize the value of the F-15, ... today the Eagle is the primary air superiority ...aft in the air forces of Japan, Saudi Arabia, and ...el.

...Today, more than twenty years after the first ...gle rolled out, it remains the world's premier air ...periority fighter, putting it in an elite class with ...er legendary fighters like the P-51 Mustang, the ...86 Sabre, and the F-4 Phantom.

General John M. Loh
Commander, Air Combat Command
1994

Chapter I
BEGINNINGS

Born of competitive hardware prototyping and head-to-head engineering competition, the F-15 Eagle, known in its beginnings as the F-X Air Superiority fighter, grew out of the Cold War 1960s. This was the period of communist expansionism in Vietnam and the regular appearance of new fighters in the Soviet inventory. The late 1960s saw the introduction of several Warsaw Pact fighters. Notable among them were the agile MiG-21, the larger, but still maneuverable MiG-23, the brute-fast, high-flying MiG-25, and the Su-15 interceptor.

This "Red Scare" was coupled with the fact that the US Air Force hadn't fielded a pure air-to-air combat fighter since the F-86 Sabre, an aircraft which made its first flight only three years following the end of World War II.

The Air Force's frontline fighter of that time was the F-4 Phantom. While this was one of the most plentiful and effective fighters of the modern US aviation era, the F-4 was actually a Navy aircraft adapted for Air Force use. It proved itself to be a multi-purpose fighter, but its effectiveness against modern Soviet aircraft was not expected by many experts to endure. In fact, the MiG-25, which could fly at Mach 3 at high altitudes, was considered nearly immune to the F-4.

US fighter development – bringing an idea through stages of concept development, full-scale development (known now as engineering and manufacturing development), to production was a process of considerable length especially when compared with the USSR. The Soviets produced itera-

With a name like Eagle, it's not surprising that its namesake was used in early illustrations. (USAF Photo)

With the performance from its Pratt & Whitney engines, which have powered all versions of the F-15, early versions of the F-15 were able to accelerate in a vertical climb. (McDonnell-Douglas Photo)

There were over five hundred different concepts for the FX, the initial designation for the F-15. This artist's concept was generally representative of those proposed and and is somewhat close to the final configuration. Note the dorsal fins which did not appear on the F-15 final design. (USAF

tions of fighter aircraft, each type of which was built only slightly different from earlier models. New US models differed significantly from early models, and, with emphasis upon higher and higher technology, development and production costs were relatively high in comparison. As a result, new US fighter aircraft were (and are) introduced infrequently.

With the view towards high tech and infrequent model introductions, the Air Force relied upon informed estimates of where foreign aircraft would be on the threat scale by the time the US fighter could be in the inventory with "rubber on the ramp."

To that end, design of the F-X Air Superiority Fighter began in 1965 with feasibility studies of what could meet the requirements of the post-1975 period.

Greatly affecting the development was the Department of Defense (DOD) trend toward aircraft system commonality among the services. Also, some DOD officials believed that the Air Force and Navy should possess a flight force of F-111, F-4, and A-7 aircraft.

The A-7 Corsair was originally a Navy aircraft but chosen by the Air Force to accomplish the close air support mission. The F-111 was a formidable, fast fighter-bomber, but again, not truly an air superiority fighter. Considerable political pressure was applied by DOD to force the Air Force to look at designing an aircraft to handle both the air-to-air and air-to-surface missions.

The original Request For Proposal (RFP) in April 1965 specified both missions and contractors responded with more than 500 designs! The typical one featured a 60,000+ pound fighter requiring exotic materials to obtain a top speed of Mach 2.7.

The Air Force, however, largely because of the work of Major John R. Boyd eventually rejected all 500 designs.

Boyd had been a fighter pilot in the late 1950s, and was the author of an air combat training manual used by the Fighter Weapons School at Nellis Air Force Base, Nevada. In 1962, Boyd was an engineering student at Georgia Tech where he studied energy changes incurred by an aircraft during flight. These studies led to methods for measuring aircraft

This 1972 production line scene shows early F-15As in production at the McDonnell-Douglas facility in St. Louis. Note the F-4 tail assemblies in the background. (McDonnell-Douglas Photo)

The early production photo shows the central fuselage and vertical stabilizers nearing completion. (McDonnell-Douglas Photo)

This 1981 production line photo shows shows early F-15Cs under production. Externally, there are no obvious differences between the F-15A and F-15C or the two-seat B or D versions. (McDonnell-Douglas Photo)

maneuverability, i.e. the ability to change altitude, airspeed, and direction.

Later, Boyd, along with Thomas Christie, a mathematician he met in his next assignment at Eglin Air Force Base, Florida, continued studies known as energy maneuverability. The pair, in May of 1964, then published an official, two-volume report on energy maneuverability theory.

Although this theory presented nothing new in terms of basic physics, it did offer designers a model against which competing F-X designs could be compared. It also made it possible to approximate the effects of design changes on aircraft performance. Using this theory, planners applied new design requirements to the F-X. By Spring 1967, the maximum weight of the concept fighter had dropped to 40,000 pounds and the top speed scaled back to a range of Mach 2.3 to 2.5. A second round of RFPs began in August 1967. Within the Air Force review team, though, there was still disagreement about the role, or roles, of the new fighter.

The multi-purpose aircraft advocates required relatively high-weight avionics to which improvements were deemed very costly and high-risk. The air superiority advocates wanted lighter weights for speed and maneuverability. The latter group eventually won out and the Required Operational Capability Statement from the Tactical Air Command left little doubt as to what the Air Force had in mind for the F-X.

But there was to be one more conceptual obstacle. Pierre M. Sprey, from the Office of Scientific Development (OSD), designed an alternative to the F-X, the F-XX. This concept had the elements of a relatively small-sized, single-piloted, single-engine 25,000 pound fighter which would do its work in the sub/transonic portion of the flight envelope. This low-cost fighter was to carry air-to-air Sidewinder missiles and a gun, and feature relatively simple avionics. Sprey further proposed a version for the Navy.

Although the Air Force and Navy rejected the F-XX concept, the YF-16/17 programs which appeared just a few years later (and which resulted in the Air Force F-16 and the Navy's F-18 fighters) seemed to bear out the merits of the "simple" lightweight fighter concept.

On December 23, 1969, at 3:30 p.m. EST, the Air Force announced McDonnell-Douglas to be the prime contractor for the F-X, which would soon pick up its famous F-15 Eagle title.

Numerous trade-off studies were run early on to determine such factors as aircraft size, swing-wing versus fixed wing, mission mix, and optimum crew size.

The F-15 from the beginning was designed with an aerial refueling capability. Notice the slight pitch-up attitude and deployed air brake which is required for this operation. (USAF Photo)

This 1986 photo shows the F-15E prototype under construction. The major modules of the aircraft are evident with the wings and tail section ready to be mated to the center fuselage section. (McDonnell-Douglas Photo)

Initial flutter problems were discovered by the F-15 prototype aircraft shown here in flight in 1972. The fix resulted in a notch on each of the horizontal stabilizers one-third of the way out from the fuselage joining point. (McDonnell-Douglas Photo)

This early F-15A, note the 1973 serial number, is devoid of all unit markings. This flight was probably a checkout or delivery flight. (USAF Photo)

The F-15 prototype (SN 10280) is shown in flight over Edwards Air Force Base in the early 1970s. (USAF Photo)

The F-15 prototype is displayed at the St Louis facility where it was manufactured. The aircraft is carrying AIM-7 Sparrows, probably dummy missiles, for this occasion. Note the stylized F-15 head-on logo immediately below the F-15 lettering on the vertical stabilizers and under the cockpit on the side of the fuselage. (McDonnell-Douglas Photo)

In the mid-1970s, the F-15 began replacing the F-4 Phantom for the air superiority mission. By the 1990s, the transition was nearly complete as the F-15 was then also given the Wild Weasel radar suppression mission which had long been accomplished by the F-4G. (USAF Photo)

The Arnold Engineering Development Center gave extensive support to the F-15 design program and verified seven design changes using its 16-foot transonic wind tunnel. Testing has continued throughout the program as changes in the aircraft or its external stores occured. (USAF Photo)

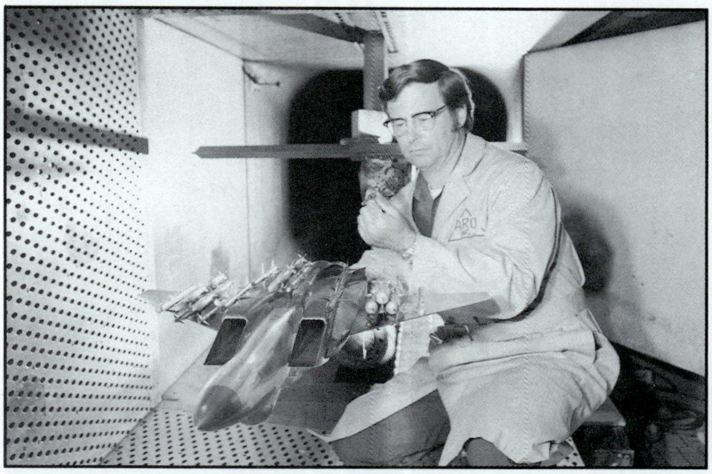

F-15 stores separation tests were conducted at the Arnold Engineering Development Center to certify safe separation of rockets, bombs, and external fuel tanks before they were actually dropped from the aircraft. This 1974 photo shows a 1/20th scale model of the F-15 with MK82 bombs and CBU-58 ordnance installed in the center's four-foot transonic wind tunnel. Through today, this facility continues to perform this important test function. (USAF Photo)

One of the more interesting aspects of F-15 flight testing involved the use of large (three-eighths scale) radio-controlled glider models of the F-15. These were launched from a NASA B-52 at Edwards Air Force Base. These tests, involving a number of these Romotely Piloted Research Vehicles, were carried out in the early 1970s. Constructed of aluminum and fiberglass, these vehicles tested the aerodynamic characteristics of the new F-15 design. They carried parachutes and were recovered in mid-air by helicopters. (USAF Photo)

Compatibility of the P&W F100 engine with the F-15's variable geometry inlet was accomplished in 1972 at the Arnold Engineering Development Center's 16-foot wind tunnel. (USAF Photo)

In January 1970, following an announcement a month earlier by F-X Program Director Major General Benjamin Bellis, McDonnell-Douglas was awarded the development contract. At that time, the F-15 program had accumulated nearly 13,000 wind tunnel hours (two years later, that sum was 23,000 hours, or four times the amount completed on the F-4).

In the same general period, Pratt & Whitney received the engine development contract over General Electric, while Hughes Aircraft Company was chosen to develop and produce the radar.

The initial contract to McDonnell-Douglas was for 20 development aircraft: a preliminary manufacture of ten single-seat F-15As (71-0280 through 71-0289); two two-seat TF-15 Category I trainers (71-0290 and 71-0291); and eight Category II Full Scale Development F-15As (72-0113 through 72-0120).

The Eagle was learning to fly.

Chapter II
HOWS & WHYS OF THE EAGLE

When the F-15 Eagle first appeared in the early 1970s, it just looked different from previous designs. Sleekness was the name of the game with this magnificent machine, and compared to the earlier F-4 and F-105, the F-15 looked like a rocket.

There were also the performance and capabilities to go along with that stylish look. The plane was built to excel in air-to-air combat and the air defense superiority missions, but in the years to come, the Eagle would also prove effective in other missions.

With its pair of powerful F100 engines, the F-15 introduced performance that was unheard-of in the 1970s. And even into the 1990s, newer versions of the aircraft still make it one of the best, if not the best, fighter in the world. Its extraordinary power enables it to accelerate in pure vertical flight and sustain extremely high G turns. The optimized aerodynamics of the Eagle provide for speeds up to Mach 2.5, along with very stable flight characteristics at high angles of attack and G loadings. Easy to understand why pilots love their Eagle!

So what makes the F-15 the fighter it is? This chapter will explain the Hows and Whys of the Eagle.

DESIGN CONSIDERATIONS

To call the F-15 a sleek machine just isn't good enough. You can almost draw a straight line from the nose to the wingtip and barely touch the tips of the intakes which stretch far forward on the fuse-

The F-15 possessed capabilities that far exceeded any earlier model aircraft. This particular F-15A is assigned to Luke Air Force Base. (USAF Photo)

This F-15A demonstrates its ability to accelerate vertically, a capability which has not been exceeded by any operational US aircraft. (USAF Photo)

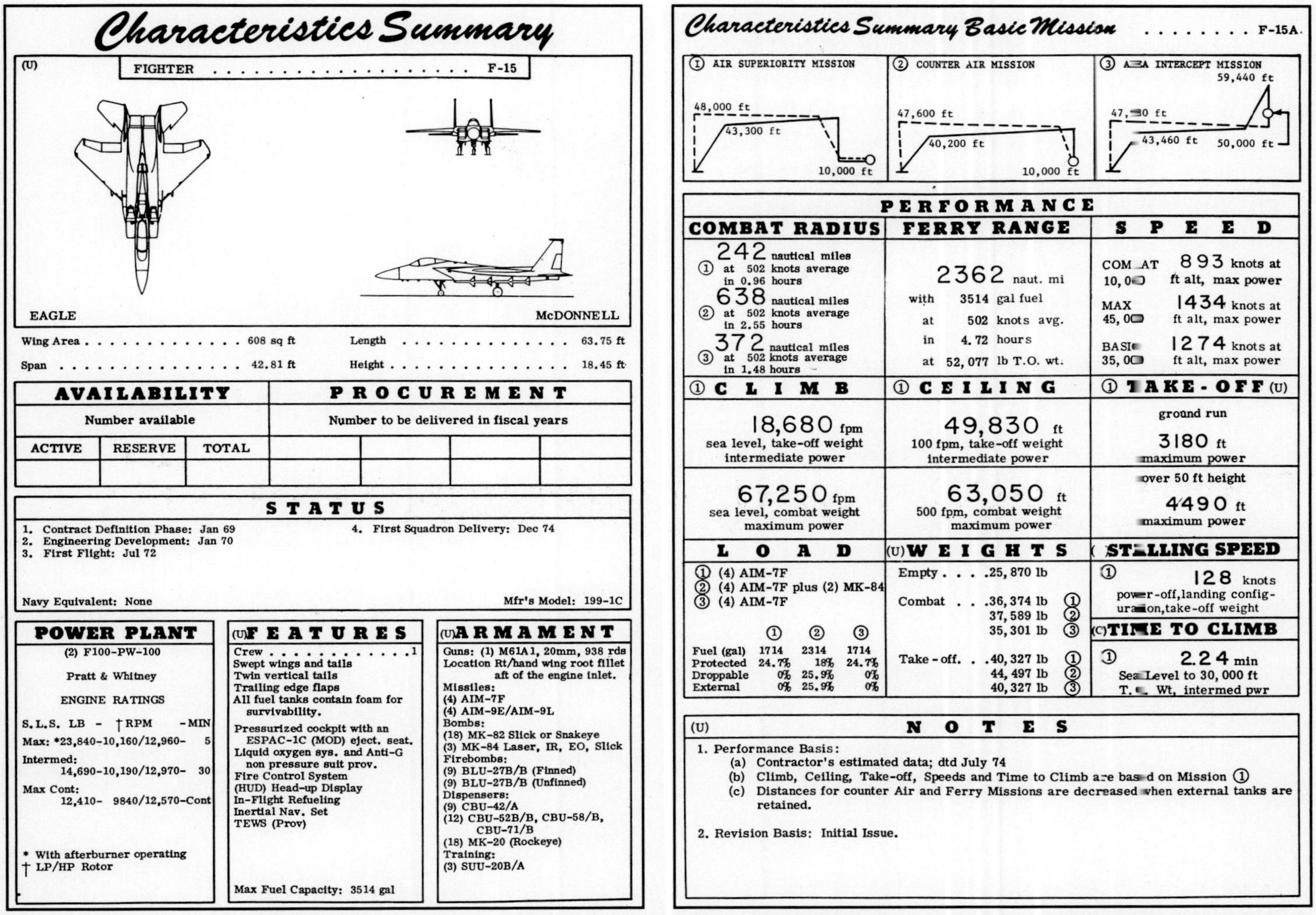

Characteristics Summary

(U) FIGHTER F-15

EAGLE — McDONNELL

Wing Area	608 sq ft	Length	63.75 ft
Span	42.81 ft	Height	18.45 ft

AVAILABILITY			PROCUREMENT			
Number available			Number to be delivered in fiscal years			
ACTIVE	RESERVE	TOTAL				

STATUS

1. Contract Definition Phase: Jan 69
2. Engineering Development: Jan 70
3. First Flight: Jul 72
4. First Squadron Delivery: Dec 74

Navy Equivalent: None — Mfr's Model: 199-1C

POWER PLANT

(2) F100-PW-100

Pratt & Whitney

ENGINE RATINGS

S.L.S. LB - †RPM - MIN

Max: *23,840-10,160/12,960- 5

Intermed: 14,690-10,190/12,970- 30

Max Cont: 12,410- 9840/12,570-Cont

* With afterburner operating

† LP/HP Rotor

(U) FEATURES

Crew 1
Swept wings and tails
Twin vertical tails
Trailing edge flaps
All fuel tanks contain foam for survivability.
Pressurized cockpit with an ESPAC-1C (MOD) eject. seat.
Liquid oxygen sys. and Anti-G non pressure suit prov.
Fire Control System
(HUD) Head-up Display
In-Flight Refueling
Inertial Nav. Set
TEWS (Prov)

Max Fuel Capacity: 3514 gal

(U) ARMAMENT

Guns: (1) M61A1, 20mm, 938 rds
Location Rt/hand wing root fillet aft of the engine inlet.
Missiles:
(4) AIM-7F
(4) AIM-9E/AIM-9L
Bombs:
(18) MK-82 Slick or Snakeye
(3) MK-84 Laser, IR, EO, Slick
Firebombs:
(9) BLU-27B/B (Finned)
(9) BLU-27B/B (Unfinned)
Dispensers:
(9) CBU-42/A
(12) CBU-52B/B, CBU-58/B, CBU-71/B
(18) MK-20 (Rockeye)
Training:
(3) SUU-20B/A

Characteristics Summary Basic Mission F-15A

PERFORMANCE

COMBAT RADIUS	FERRY RANGE	SPEED
① 242 nautical miles at 502 knots average in 0.96 hours ② 638 nautical miles at 502 knots average in 2.55 hours ③ 372 nautical miles at 502 knots average in 1.48 hours	2362 naut. mi with 3514 gal fuel at 502 knots avg. in 4.72 hours at 52,077 lb T.O. wt.	COMBAT 10,000 893 knots at ft alt, max power MAX 45,000 1434 knots at ft alt, max power BASIC 35,000 1274 knots at ft alt, max power

① CLIMB	① CEILING	① TAKE-OFF (U)
18,680 fpm sea level, take-off weight intermediate power	49,830 ft 100 fpm, take-off weight intermediate power	ground run 3180 ft maximum power
67,250 fpm sea level, combat weight maximum power	63,050 ft 500 fpm, combat weight maximum power	over 50 ft height 4490 ft maximum power

LOAD

① (4) AIM-7F
② (4) AIM-7F plus (2) MK-84
③ (4) AIM-7F

	①	②	③
Fuel (gal)	1714	2314	1714
Protected	24.7%	18%	24.7%
Droppable	0%	25.9%	0%
External	0%	25.9%	0%

(U) WEIGHTS

Empty	25,870 lb	
Combat	36,374 lb	①
	37,589 lb	②
	35,301 lb	③
Take-off	40,327 lb	①
	44,497 lb	②
	40,327 lb	③

(U) STALLING SPEED

① 128 knots
power-off, landing configuration, take-off weight

(C) TIME TO CLIMB

① 2.24 min
Sea Level to 30,000 ft
T.O. Wt, intermed pwr

(U) NOTES

1. Performance Basis:
   (a) Contractor's estimated data; dtd July 74
   (b) Climb, Ceiling, Take-off, Speeds and Time to Climb are based on Mission ①
   (c) Distances for counter Air and Ferry Missions are decreased when external tanks are retained.
2. Revision Basis: Initial Issue.

This official Characteristics Summary of the F-15A provides listing of the capabilities and power characteristics of the aircraft. (USAF Chart)

The center fuselage and wing areas provide significant weapons-carriage locations. Through the various models of the F-15, this location has seen a multitude of air-to-air, air-to-ground, ASAT, and both dumb and smart bombs. (USAF Photo)

lage. The plane looks like a dagger and for any adversary of the Eagle, that look is enacted into action with the same intention.

Sizewise, the F-15 is considerably larger than the F-4 Phantom it replaced. But with more efficient fuel packaging, the F-15 amazingly weighs less based on F-15A and F-4C empty weights. Some of the weight efficiency was obtained from the use of here-to-fore unused advanced (for the time period) materials. An amazing one-quarter of the Eagle's weight is super-strong titanium. Much of that exotic material is located around the engines and inboard sections. The twin vertical tails of the F-15 also use a boron composite material.

For production purposes, the Eagle can be divided into four major pieces: the nose section which contains the radome, canopy and nose landing gear; the central fuselage carrying the jet intakes, main landing gear and serving as the attachment location for the wings; the wings themselves; and the rear fuselage section containing the propulsion system and the attachment points for the four rear tail surfaces.

The F-15 configuration features outboard ailerons (which provide the primary aircraft flight control) and which have a plus-or-minus 20 degree deflection. The horizontal stabilizers provide for pitch and roll control. All the flight surfaces are deflected hydraulically.

It was surprising to some at the time the F-15 didn't carry the swingwing design of the F-14 or F-111. There are movable surfaces, though, as the air inlets can be adjusted in flight for varying angle-of-attack and Mach conditions.

The consideration at the time of design was that most dogfighters didn't exceed speeds over Mach one. Thus, it was decided that the complications of a swing wing would be deleted, giving up some loiter time capabilities, but also deleting a lot of complicated hardware, and obviously, a lot of extra weight.

Don't let the fact that this is a fighter aircraft deceive you. This is a big aircraft with a wingspan of almost 43 feet and an overall length of almost 64 feet, the size of a World War II medium bomber. (McDonnell-Douglas Photo)

The F-15 is the sum of its parts as shown in this photo. The main parts of this F-15C are the nose section, the central wing box assembly, the wings themselves, and the rear fuselage section. (McDonnell-Douglas Photo)

This F-15 production clearly illustrates the location and functioning of the top-fuselage-mounted drag brake. The hydraulically operated unit is used during landing and for aerial maneuvers. (McDonnell-Douglas Photo)

This 1985 test photo shows the application of various simulated flight loads at the McDonnell Aircraft in St. Louis. This particular test involved F-15 tail sections constructed of composite and titanium materials to demonstrate the weight and cost advantages of these materials. This type of testing goes on continuously during the operational lifetime of the aircraft in order to determine potential structural problems. (USAF Photo)

As it finally worked out, the only variable geometry features on the F-15 are its engine inlets which can be directed from four degrees above level to 11 degrees below level to ensure adequate airflow, especially during high angle-of-attack maneuvers. These moveable inlets also allow a reduction in the size of the stabilizers, or horizontal tail structures.

STRUCTURE

Although advanced technology played heavily in other portions of the aircraft, the airframe itself is a conventional design. Exotic materials, though, are used in abundance with titanium and graphite receiving great use in this aircraft.

Wing loading was a heavy criterian in the F-15 airframe design. Making it as minimal as possible was the goal, and what resulted was an impressive 68 pounds per square feet wing loading with a full fuel load. A 50 percent reduction in internal fuel reduces the figure to 57 pounds per square feet. With a thrust-to-weight ratio of 1.4-to-1 with a half load of fuel, it's easy to understand the outstanding performance of the F-15.

From previous fighter design studies and inputs from experienced pilots, visibility enjoyed a high priority in the design phase. No problem with the

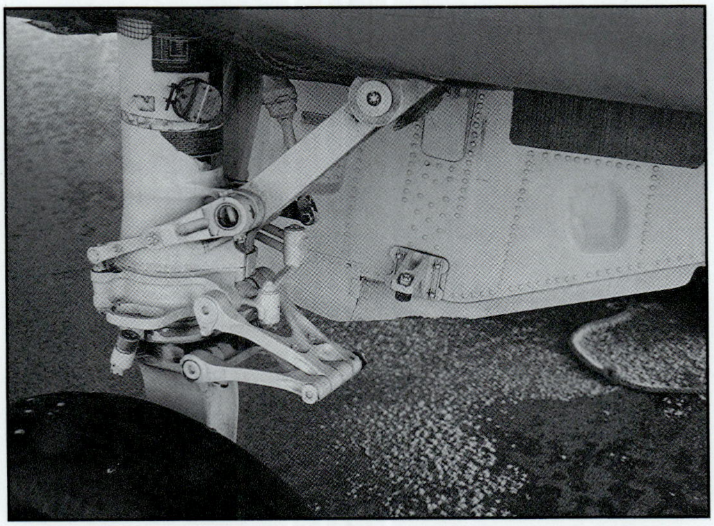

This photo shows the complex front landing gear for the F-15. It has to be tough to accept the load from a 40,000+ aircraft hitting the runway at 200+ knots. The gear is also steerable and serves as the point of connection for towing the aircraft. (Bill Holder Photo)

Every new USAF aircraft model gets to spend some time in one of two Air Force's large anechoic chambers. This F-15C, at Eglin Air Force Base facility, is undergoing electromagnetic compatibility testing. (USAF Photo)

Eagle as there is nothing but "The Wild Blue" in every direction. That canopy is super strong, being constructed of space-age polycarbonate and capable of taking a four-pound bird strike at 335 knots. You'll notice that the canopy many times stays down as the aircraft is rolling on the ramp. The pilots of this machine will tell you that one of the creature comforts of the Eagle is its great air conditioning systems.

From a survivability point of view, redundancy is incorporated in the structure. For example, one vertical tail, or one of its three wing spars can be severed without causing loss of the aircraft. Redundancy is also evident in the fuel system which incorporates self-sealing features and foam lining to inhibit fires and explosions. Also, the combined hydraulic and mechanical flight control systems is backed by a fly-by-wire capability to increase survivability.

The F-15 ejection seat, the ACES II, is a pilot's best friend and is capable of ejection at up to 600 knots. The rocket-powered trajectory is stabilized by the DART alignment system.

But even with all the performance considerations, the designers had to play with, the mechanics on the line were certainly remembered with this aircraft. For example, the lubrication points were reduced by over 300 from the F-4, along with a number other maintenance-easing innovations.

POWERPLANT

Survivability was a heavy requirement in the design of the Eagle. Right off the bat, it's nice to have two engines should one decide to quit functioning. Thus, the decision was made to make the F-15 a dual-engine fighter.

A vigorous powerplant competition took place in the late 1960s between General Electric and Pratt & Whitney for the lucrative contract. In 1970, the P&W design was declared the winner with the powerplant being a giant step forward in technology.

The winning F100 engine had three main goals-high thrust capabilities, light weight, and low fuel consumption. Even though those three goals seem to be conflicting, all three were accomplished.

The maximum thrust capability of the engine is in the 15,000 pound thrust range (without afterburner) with an additional 10,000 pounds with the A/B. The engine swallows an amazing 860 pounds of

This photo depicts the inboard right view of the rear fuselage section. Mounting both the vertical and horizontal stabilizers, the area absorbs extremely large loading without deflection. (Bill Holder Photo)

One of the most visible aspects of the F-15 design are the huge slanted variable-flow intakes. This radical styling served as the basis for a number of other late-model fighters which would follow. Note that intakes are slightly separated from the fuselage, i.e. not flared into the fuselage like earlier aircraft. (Bill Holder Photo)

A head-on shot showing lower fuselage details with the front and main landing gears and engine intakes. Again, note the separated engine inlets which seem to pull away from the lower fuselage. (Bill Holder Photo)

The Electronic Warfare Warning Antenna is located on the port side of the rear fuselage section. An identical installation is located on the other side of the aircraft. (Bill Holder Photo)

This pod configuration is located atop both vertical stabilizers. The starboard unit contains electronic counter-measures, the port-side unit contains warning components. (Bill Holder Photo)

Looking at the hot end of an F-15, the exhaust nozzles from its pair of Pratt & Whitney F100 powerplants, each capable of 25,000 pounds of thrust with afterburners cooking! (Bill Holder Photo)

Additional range was an early consideration for the F-15. To accomplish this goal, conformal fuel tanks were developed by the contractor and built at its Tulsa, Oklahoma facility. Each conformal fuel tank carries five thousand pounds of fuel and was designed to produce minimum drag. Unlike the center-mounted tank, these tanks could not be jettisoned. They would later be incorporated on all F-15Es. (both - McDonnell-Douglas Photo)

fuel per minute when operating in the afterburner mode.

The F100 is defined as a low-bypass ratio turbofan engine with a ten-stage compressor having a pressure ratio 8-1 and an overall pressure ratio of 25-1.

A number of improvements have been made to the basic F-15 powerplant (the F100-PW-100) over the years with follow-on designations being the F100-PW-200, F100-PW-220, and F100-PW-229 versions. The -220 version demonstrated a 99 percent readiness capability during the Desert Storm confrontation. That latest 229 version was first incorporated in 1991.

The canopy of this F-15B is shown in the full-up position. The only disruptions to vision is the single support rib. Also, the close proximity of the top of the engine inlet. (McDonnell-Douglas Photo)

The aft end of this early F-15A is being mated the wing and forward fuselage section at the McDonnell-Douglas plant in St. Louis. Emphasizing the size of this aircraft is a number of technicians nearly lost in the detail. (USAF Photo)

Maneuverability was certainly a design goal with the Eagle as can be seen by the large control surface area. Also note the hydraulically-activated drag brake in the fully-extended position. (McDonnell-Douglas Photo)

It's obvious that aerodynamics played heavily in the contouring of the upper fuselage shape. The body was "area-ruled" for supersonic flight, someth ng this bird does quite well. (McDonnell-Douglas Photo)

The F100-PW-220 engine, which is mostly used on the C and D models, was also in competition with the General Electric F110-GE-100 for the F-16. That heated competition, by the way, was known as "The Great Engine War." (Pratt & Whitney Photo)

Looking at the business end of the pair of F100 engines. The exhaust nozzles are shown in the fully-retracted position. With afterburner, each of these engines is worth about 25,000 pounds of thrust. This powerplant is virtually identical to the engine used in F-16As and Bs. (USAF Photo)

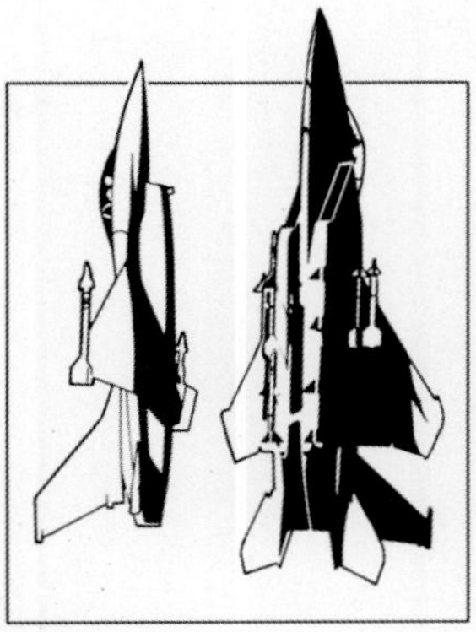

F100-PW-100

Winner of intense competition in the early 1970s to power the U.S. Air Force's new air superiority fighter, the F-15 Eagle.

F100-PW-200

A version of the F100-PW-100 designed for single-engine aircraft, entered service in the mid-1970s powering the U. S. Air Force's lightweight fighter, the F-16 Fighting Falcon.

F100-PW-220

Based on lessons learned, incorporates the latest technology available in the 1980s for both F-15s and F-16s, providing increased reliability, durability, operability and ease of maintenance. It has achieved the best safety record in U. S. Air Force history.

UNITED TECHNOLOGIES PRATT&WHITNEY

F100-PW-220E

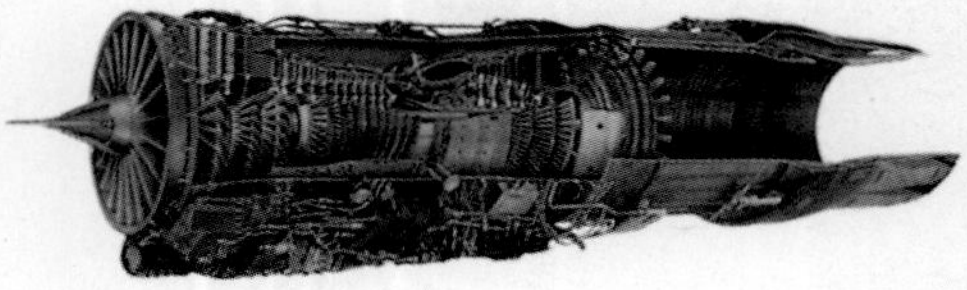

Earlier F100-PW-100 and F100-PW-200 engines can be upgraded to achieve the level of technology of the F100-PW-220. This configuration is termed the F100-PW-220E, "E" standing for equivalent.

F100-PW-229

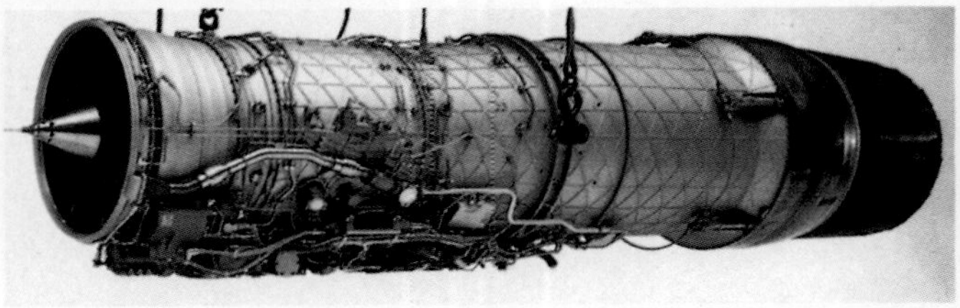

The most advanced production model in the F100 family, providing a significant performance improvement and the latest technology available for the l990s. It can be installed in all F-15 and F- 16 aircraft.

F100-PW-220+/E+

The technology of the F100-PW-229 can also be incorporated into earlier F100 engines to enhance safety, reliability and performance. This configuration is known as the F100-PW-220+ or F100-PW-220E+.

At the McDonnell-Douglas assembly line, this F100 engine is ready to be installed in an F-15. Interestingly, the engine (as well as the radar) was government-furnished equipment by virtue of a separate prime contract with Pratt & Whitney. (McDonnell-Douglas Photo)

AVIONICS

The almost all-digital avionics system of the F-15 is the brain of this magnificent machine. The system is unique in the way it is integrated with the weapon systems.

The front end of the avionics system is the 36-inch diameter radar which is carried under the front radome. This radar gives the pilot the capability to locate, track, and fire against both high- and low-flying aircraft at distances beyond 50 miles with extraordinary accuracy. The pilot will then know where the target is, where it is going, and what must be done to maneuver into the most advantageous position to engage. The information is then passed on to the weapon systems.

PREVIOUS: This figure presents the "family tree" of F100 engines which have been used in both the F-15 and F-16 aircraft. Only the -200 and -220 versions were in the F-16. (Pratt & Whitney Photo)

The information is displayed to the pilot in the cockpit on his Heads-Up Display, or HUD. This high-tech monitor helps the pilot visually locate, identify, and engage the enemy aircraft by encircling it in a target designator box.

The launching of the appropriate weapon systems is accomplished by the Weapon Delivery System. Major components include an altitude and heading reference system, the ILS Landing System, and the UHF Communications system. These complex systems are all interlinked by the Central Computer.

The Eagle also carries a sophisticated Identification Friend or Foe (IFF) system. This unit enables the Eagle to electronically interrogate aircraft at

Shown during a maintenance inspection, this F-15 has its front radome hinged to the starboard side for ease of maintenance. The "wings" on the forward fuselage are lifted providing access to electronics and hydraulics. (USAF Photo)

great distances to determine which side the aircraft is on.

One of the Eagle's most high-tech systems is the so-called TEWS (Tactical Electronic Warfare System), which is receiving a substantial update in the 1990s. Major components in the TEWS system include the Internal Countermeasures Set, Radar Warning Receiver, the Chaff/Flare Dispenser.

The Central Computer, of course, is the nerve center of the F-15 electronics suite, but valuable data is also provided by the Air Data Computer. This computer acquires aircraft position data from a number of sources and then provides the resulting data back to the cockpit instruments.

The F-15 is most often denoted as an air-superiority aircraft-that's obviously the way it was designed-and where most of its capability lies. But if you look at the air-to-ground ordnance the plane can carry, you quickly ascertain that the Eagle also

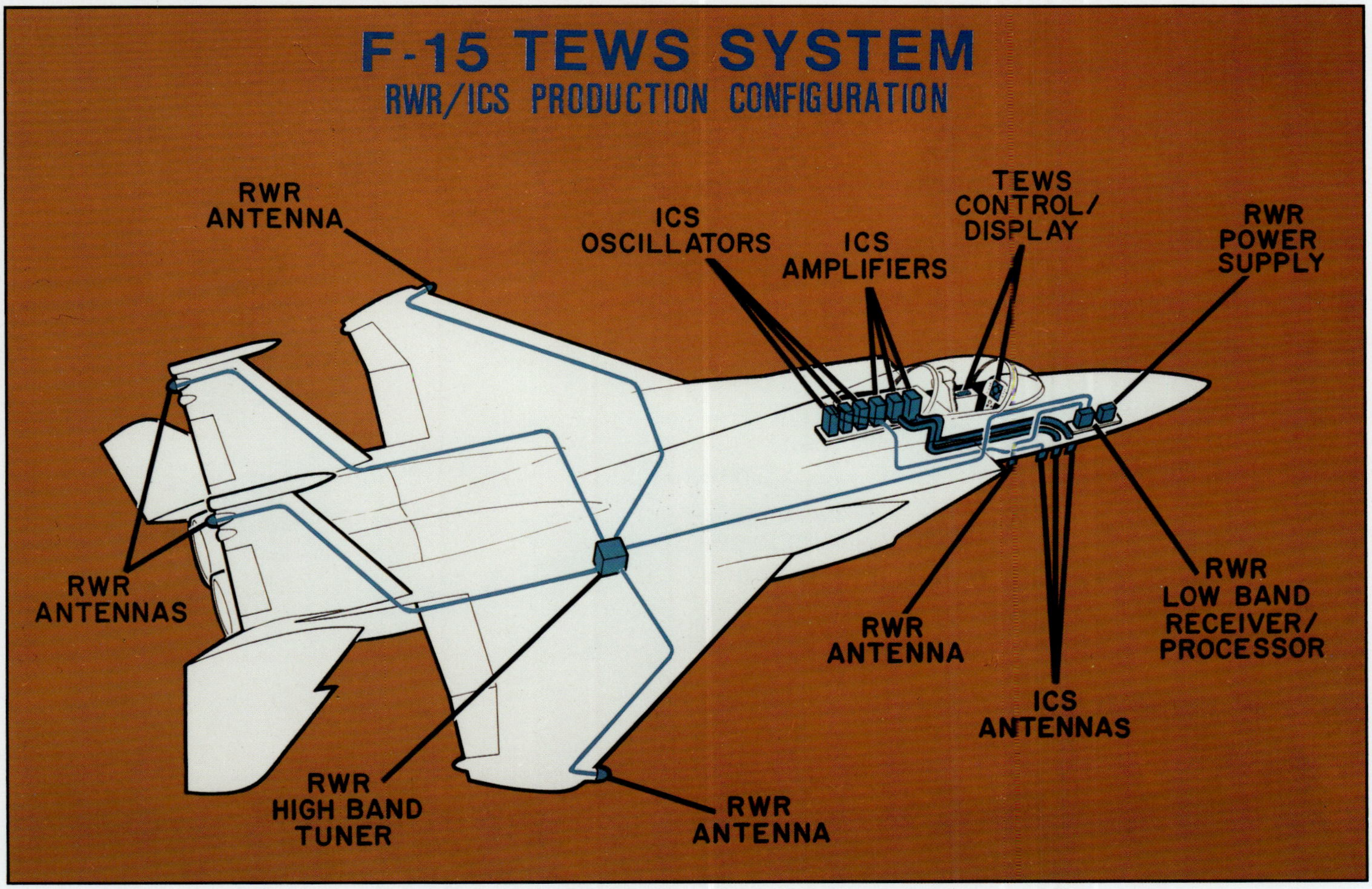

The main components of the Tactical Electronic Warfare System (TEWS) are shown by this drawing. This system basically detects, confuses and defeats enemy radar systems. (USAF Photo)

The nearly-unobstructed, practically undistorted view of the pilot of this F-15B is something to behold. Directly in front of the pilot's eyes, and in this picture, visible just to the right of the helmet is the F-15's head-up display. This system enables the pilot to acquire threat and navigation information without ever lowering his eyes. (McDonnell-Douglas Photo)

carries a significant ground attack capability, and it certainly has the electronic capability to handle that mission as well.

ARMAMENT

When fighters were first designed, the prime method of defense (and offense) was guns. But with the advent of air-to-air missiles, however, many felt the day of the gun was over. But the Vietnam experience proved that the concept was still very viable. Hence, the Eagle has guns, actually make that "gun." It is the General Electric M61A1 Vulcan 20mm system, a rotary Gatling gun with the capability to fire at the rate of six thousand rounds per minute. The awesome system uses six barrels and a linkless feed system.

Totally loaded, the Vulcan system weighs 935 pounds, with only 235 pounds being the gun weight. The system is capable of firing three types of ammunition – API (M53), HEI (M56), and HEIT (M242). Recently, the Air Force has also adopted the use of a new ammunition for the Vulcan, known as the PGU-28/B Semi-Armor Piercing High-Explosive Incendiary (SAPHEI) ammunition which has greatly increased capabilities. The same system is also used as the tail stinger on the B-52H.

OPPOSITE: These F-15Cs, configured in an air defense mode, are carrying four AIM-9 Sidewinder heat-seeking missiles on the underwing pylons. On the fuselage pylons are four AIM-7 Sparrow missiles. Note that these Eagles are going straight up even carrying the drag-inducing externally-mounted missiles. (McDonnell-Douglas Photo)

Gun systems through the years have been symmetrical devices, usually located along the centerline of the fuselage, or located in the same position on each wing. Several fuselage gun locations were considered for the F-15 with the location finally being selected as the starboard wing root.

But even though the gun is present, recent combat experience in Desert Storm also showed the importance of air-to-air missiles in aerial combat. The two prime missiles include the AIM-7 Sparrow and the AIM-9 Sidewinder, both of which have been modified many times.

The AIM-7 has an illustrious history actually beginning life in the mid-1950s as the Navy AAM-N-2. Initially as beam-rider system, the AIM-7C evolved in the early 1960s as a radar homing missile. Early versions of the F-15 carried the AIM-7E which carries a continuous rod warhead. The AIM-7F is

This F-15A, from the 48th FIS, fires an AIM-7 Sparrow radar-guided missile in a test flight. Clean ordnance separation as depicted here, would be a concern later with early F-15E missile firings tests. (McDonnell-Douglas Photo)

the current configuration, a superb performer in Desert Storm.

The AIM-7F's guidance system has solid state electronics and a 60+ mile range. The more powerful solid fuel propulsion system pushes an 88 pound warhead to the target.

The Sidewinder, for example, has a superior seeker head, giving the Eagle the ability to shoot down targets form all angles using a heat-seeking missile. In the early 1990s, there was also a serious consideration for the development of an AIM-9X missile which could replace the current AIM-9M in the future.

The AIM-9 is another longtime performer with the development roots stretching back to the late 1940s time period. The early 1990s 9L version is the third generation of this infrared-seeking missile. Various versions of the Sidewinder have seen action with most American combat aircraft through the years. With the F-15, it's certainly been a winner.

A recent addition to the air-to-air armament for the F-15 is the AIM-120 Advanced Medium Range Air-To-Air Missile (AMRAAM) missile. This system was designed to allow several targets to be engaged simultaneously, and enable a "launch and leave" concept. The AIM-120 (which was certified in September 1991) will be a standard weapon for the F-15 and other aircraft into the next century. New versions of the AMRAAM are also being considered, which could be fitted to F-15s in the middle and late 1990s.

This test aircraft, note the fluorescent pylons and paint patches, carries the AGM-130A missile for a test firing. (USAF Photo)

Besides its air-to-air ordnance, this F-15A also sports the centerline 610 gallon, 3960 pound external fuel tank. The F-15 can also carry two additional tanks, one under each wing which enables the Eagle to carry an amazing 32,000 pounds of fuel (three external tanks plus all internal fuel). (USAF Photo)

During the aircraft's first flight test involving a live "Smart Weapon", an F-15E launches an AGM-65B TV-guided Maverick missile. The test demonstrated that the F-15E's advanced radar and infrared sensor systems could quickly and precisely locate small tactical targets. (McDonnell-Douglas Photo)

Above: This photo shows another test aircraft carrying the AGM-130A missile. (USAF Photo) Below: Captive carry tests of an AGM-88 HARM missile is carried out aboard the same F-15E at Eglin Air Force Base, Florida in 1992. The test evaluated the compatibility of the aircraft and the missile. This was one of a ten-flight program. This aircraft was attached to the 3246th Test Wing at Eglin. (McDonnell-Douglas Photo)

The Eagle is capable of carrying its air-to-air missile suite in addition to a multitude of ground attack missiles, rockets and bombs. One of these systems is the anti-radiation HARM missile has proved to be a very effective system against ground radar targets.

The Maverick AGM-65 air-to-ground missile is designed to acquire and destroy small point targets such as tanks, armored personnel carriers and bunkers, and larger targets such as factories, ships and bridges. When coupled with the LANTIRN system of the later version F-15E, the Maverick can acquire targets at greater distances. Once electronically "locked on", the Maverick has a nine-to-one probability of hitting its target. Another heavy-hitting ordnance carried by the F-15 is the AGM-130, which is a rocket-powered version of the GBU-15 guided bomb. The weapon weighs 2,950 pounds and is a startling 156 inches in length. Both the AGM-130 and GBU-15 are "smart" weapons Their on-board computers use information such as speed, altitude and target location from the F-15's computer to guide their trajectories with pinpoint accuracy.

A tactical version of the Short Range Attack Missile (SRAM) missile was also considered as a weapon for the F-15 with tests carried out at Edwards Air Force Base in 1991. The so-called SRAM T was to be integrated with the F-15E, but the program was never carried forward.

The weapons which could be carried by early versions of the F-15 are displayed in front of this early F-15B. Shown are the various missiles (both air-to-air and air-to-ground), bombs, gun ammunition. Additional weapons were incorporated into the F-15E. (USAF Photo)

This F-15E is loaded to the hilt with both air-to-air Sidewinder missiles and MK-20 Rockeye II cluster bombs. (McDonnell-Douglas Photo)

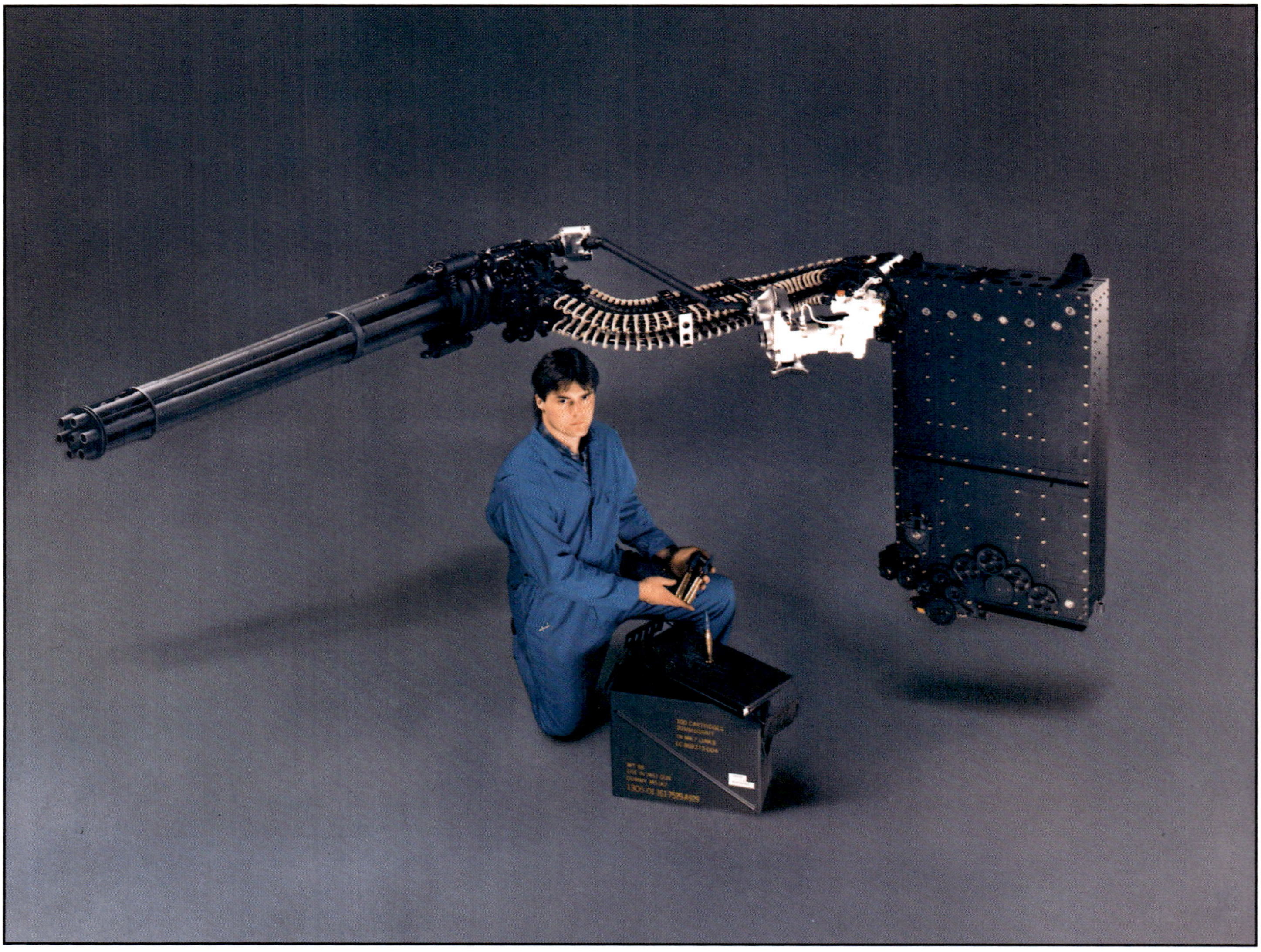

The immense size of the M61A1 weapon system is illustrated by comparison with technician. The case to the right side of the photo holds the ammunition (a total of 500 rounds) which alone weighs 282 pounds! The entire system weighs 770 pounds. (General Electric Photo)

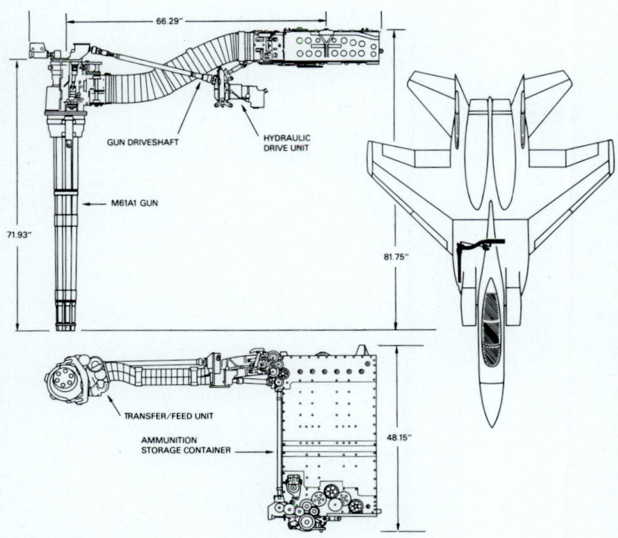

CHARACTERISTICS

Gun	M61A1, 20-mm
Weight	
Feed System	236 lbs.
Gun	252 lbs.
Ammunition	282 lbs.
Total	770 lbs.
Firing Rate	4000 & 6000 spm (Pilot Option)
Ammunition Capacity	500 rounds
Feed System	Linear, Double ended, controlled conveyor elements, closed loop
Drive System	Hydraulic
Power Requirements	
@ 6000 spm	29.0 gpm @ 2600 psi Δ P
@ 4000 spm	19.5 gpm @ 2000 psi Δ P
Ammunition	PGU-28/B Saphei, M50 Series, 20-mm
Reliability	23,000 MRBF
Scheduled Maintenance	30,000 rounds
System Life	100,000 rounds
Firing Position	4 o'clock looking fwd.
Acceleration Time	Less than 0.5 sec. to 6000 spm
Deceleration Time	Less than 0.5 sec. from 6000 spm

The characteristics of the awesome M61A1 20mm Gatling Gun are shown by this table. (General Electric Table)

Although initially designed as an air superiority fighter, the Eagle also has acquired a significant ground attack capability. Here this Luke AFB F-15E dispenses 12 MK-82 500 pound bombs in a 1989 test. (McDonnell-Douglas Photo)

MAINTENANCE

The F-15 is an aircraft designed and built with maintenance in mind from the very beginning. When a component of the aircraft needs repair, ground crews can remove it quickly, replace it with a spare, and repair the broken piece in specially designed maintenance areas. Even the F100 engine is comprised of five modules, each being interchangeable from one engine to another.

USAF F-15s are maintained by the Warner Robbins Air Logistics Center, Georgia. At any one time, some three dozen F-15s are undergoing the strenuous maintenance process.

At Warner Robbins, F-15s go through a 120 day Programmed Depot Maintenance (PDM) process. During the process, the aircraft is stripped of wings and engines and checked down to the last rivet. PDM also brings each F-15 back to Warner Robbins

Warner Robbins Air Logistics Center, Robbins Air Force Base, Georgia is the location for depot-level maintenance for F-15s worldwide. The F-15 was the first major Air Force weapon system to fall under the new Air Force "cradle-to-grave" management concept. F-15s go through a 120 day Programmed Depot Maintenance (PDM) process. The process involves comprehensive maintenance including the stripping of wings and engines, certainly a major overall of the highest order. (USAF Photo)

AF
84004
EG

OPPOSITE: Performance is the keynote with the F-15. With its great thrust-to-weight capabilities, the Eagle has demonstrated a climb to over 98,000 feet in less than three and one half minutes. Here, an F-15C from the 33 TFG at Eglin does its thing. (USAF Photo)

every six years for a major structural overhaul. A number of F-15s have also gone through the so-called Multi-Stage Improvement Program at the same time, a process which involves installation of new wiring and avionics along with extensive cockpit display technology upgrades.

PERFORMANCE

The F-15 was a giant step forward in performance over previous fighter aircraft. There's the old rule that the lower the wing loading, the more maneuverability an aircraft possesses. And as was stated earlier, the Eagle's ultra-low loading enables it to turn on a dime.

Add the fact that the Eagle has the punch from its pair of powerful engines to push the plane through those tight maneuvers, and you can see why the craft is so admired. With its greater-than-one thrust-to-weight ratio at combat weight, the Eagle had unique capabilities when it was first introduced. The Eagle can climb like a rocket, and has demonstrated a climb to over 98,000 feet in less that three and one-half minutes with the modified Streak Eagle research aircraft.

The fact that the F-15 is able to fly over its design G loading was an early area of concern to the Air Force. A system coined the Overload Warning System now warns F-15 pilots when the dangerous situation occurs. The system was retrofitted into all F-15s in the mid-1980s, with all later production Eagles carrying the system.

F-15 pilots hear a female voice repeating "Over G, Over G!" when the Eagle is flown near the craft's structural limit. The system is activated when the aircraft reaches 85 percent of its limit loading. At 92 percent, the tone changes, and at 100 percent, the voice message is continuously announced until the loading is reduced to acceptable limits.

These F-15Cs are tucked together in formation carrying air-to-air missile loads. Note the nozzle (muzzle opening) for the M61A1 20mm cannon on the rightwing glove. The opening is located slightly aft of the right intake to eliminate possible stall-producing gas ingestion problems. Firing the gun causes no flight stability problems. (McDonnell-Douglas Photo)

The over-600 square feet in wing area provides the F-15 with significant lift during take-offs and equally-large drag during landing enabling the aircraft to use extremely short runways. This capability is certainly a significant attribute for an aircraft this size. (USAF Photo)

Chapter III
EAGLE VERSIONS

The first F-15 rolled out at the McDonnell Aircraft facility in St. Louis, June 26, 1972. The contractor then disassembled the aircraft and sent it, via a USAF C-5 Galaxy, to the Air Force Flight Test Center, Edwards Air Force Base, California for reassembly, checkout, and preparation for the first test flight which occured shortly thereafter. McDonnell-Douglas Chief Test Pilot, Irving Burrows, took the aircraft (71-02809) on that maiden flight.

One of the front lines of air defense during the Cold War were F-15A's based at Elmendorf Air Force Base in Alaska. These Eagles were the 21st TFW. In this tough weather environment, the F-15 certainly demonstrated the cold end of the all-weather capability. (McDonnell-Douglas Photo)

This F-15B, with special camouflage paint, was modified with conformal tanks for the so-called Dual Role Fighter, which would eventually become the F-15E. (USAF Photo)

The first two-seater flew initially on July 7, 1973, and was later used for trainer evaluation. It is interesting to note that the first TF-15A was produced between the seventh and eighth F-15A and, throughout early production, every seventh Eagle was a two-seater B version. Also early on, the "TF-15" designation would be dropped in favor of the "F-15B" nomenclature.

The F-15A, the first of the Eagle breed, was produced from 1973 through 1979 for a total of 384. (McDonnell-Douglas Photo)

All F-15s are similar in exterior appearance. Each is nearly 64 feet in length and 10.5 feet in height, with a 42 foot wingspan. Its twin tails are tipped – starboard side with an electronic countermeasures pod and port side with a radar warning components pod.

The F-15A was one of the first Air Force production fighters to made extensive use of light and super-strong titanium – 28.8% of the airframe. The material is difficult to machine and McDonnell-Douglas had to develop special manufacturing processes for it. Other technologies used by the con-

Flat out performance has been an F-15 forté from the very beginning. This F-15A, from Luke Air Force Base, pours on the power in a straight-up climb. Note that this particular Eagle is performing the climb carrying the centerline 610 gallon external tank. (USAF Photo)

OPPOSITE: The F-15A cockpit featured analog displays. With its two engines and air-to-air capabilities, the pilot's job was very complex. The complexity can certainly be noted from the number of dials and instruments. It should be noted that the F-15E's cockpit would be completely different with an emphasis of digital displays. The MSIP Program would also introduce digital upgrades to F-15C and D models in the 1980s. (McDonnell-Douglas Photo)

tractor for the F-15 included computerized pipe bending, robot drilling, and laser cutting.

The tail surfaces of the F-15 are fabricated of boron epoxy composites while the bulkheads are of titanium. The speed brake is graphite composite skin over an aluminum honeycomb core. Composites are made of fibers "set" in a matrix material which binds the fibers together. Very lightweight composites are extremely strong, their strengths tailored by putting layers of them on top of each other while alternating each layer's fiber direction very similar to plywood.

One of the Air Force's early considerations for the F-15 was a swing wing configuration. This concept, though, was rejected ultimately with the only variable features being its engine inlets which can be directed from four degrees above and 11 degrees below the level position. The capability ensures adequate airflow, especially during high

The F-15 has long been a mainstay of European defense. These 1977-vintage F-15As are on patrol with the 32nd TFS from Soesterberg Air Base in the Netherlands. Since that time, all other models (C, D, and E) have seen European service. (USAF Photo)

Although capable of flying right down on the deck, this F-15A is at a relatively high altitude. The apparent shadow underneath the plane is a lake which gives the impression of the plane being about ten feet in the air. The Eagle is good, but not that good! (McDonnell-Douglas Photo)

The 6th Fighter Wing has been a longtime user of the F-15, here shown with 1976 F-15As over a cold European landscape. Later, this same organization would score many kills in Desert Storm with F-15Es. (USAF Photo)

The F-15B shown here was produced in considerably fewer numbers than the A version with 61 being produced. Of course, the prime purpose of this configuration was for training, check-out, and certification of pilots. (USAF Photo)

angle-of-attack maneuvering. These moveable inlets (although not able to be controlled from the cockpit) also provide additional flight control surfaces which allow a reduction in the size of the stabilizers, or horizontal tail structures.

There currently are five USAF F-15 designations: A, B, C, D, and E. The "B" is a two-seat version of the "A", while the "D" is a two-seat version of the "C." The "E" is a version which, ironically, fulfills an original requirement for both air-to-air and air-to-surface capabilities. The F-15E requires a crew of two – pilot and weapons system officer.

In addition, F-15C/Ds were extensively modified under the Multi-State Improvement Program (MSIP) with the rollout of the initial MSIP F-15C taking place in June 1985. There were 118 MSIP F-15s built.

There also are foreign F-15s. The first foreign nation to acquire F-15s (A-D models) was Israel in December 1976. Japan accepted delivery of its initial F-15s (C/D models), designated F-15Js and F-15DJs, in 1980. Japan began producing its own F-15s under special licensing arrangements the following year. Deliveries to Saudia Arabia of C/D models began in January 1981. A second buy was planned during the 1990s for 72 additional E models, initially designated F-15XL, and later F-15S. (See Chapter IV for additional foreign F-15 details).

This late production F-15C sits in front of the main hangar of its builder, McDonnell-Douglas at St Louis. It's interesting to note that there is not noticeable external difference between the F-15A and C, or for that matter, the B and D. (McDonnell-Douglas Photo)

The F-15C was a much heavier bird than the initial Eagle. In fact, the overall weight increased from about 56,000 pounds to a bulky 68,000 pounds. Landing gear strengthening was required to accommodate the additional weight. (McDonnell-Douglas Photo)

Sizable electronic improvements were made to the F-15C/D versions with the major portion being made to the radar system. The memory capacity of the onboard computer was quadrupled over the F-15A/B to 96K. This particular Eagle is assigned to the 33rd Fighter Wing at Eglin Air Force Base. (McDonnell-Douglas Photo)

F-15A/B

Designed as an air-to-air killer from the beginning, the F-15A is a Mach 2.5 class fighter. Its two Pratt & Whitney engines (F100-PW-100) each produce a maximum 25,000 pounds of thrust. This thrust, when combined with a relatively light total weight of approximately 56,000 gross takeoff weight, provides the F-15A with excellent maneuverability and acceleration. For its era, this first Eagle was eons ahead of its time.

The two-seat F-15B carries about 2,000 pounds less fuel than the "A" due to the larger instructor-pilot/student pilot cockpit. Otherwise, the models are practically identical.

F-15C/D

F-15C/Ds began delivery after June 1976. C/Ds carried additional fuel internally and had modifications to the landing gear, tires, and brake mechanisms which allowed for an increase of 12,000 pounds in maximum takeoff weight over A/B models.

These models also incorporated a radar-programmable signal processor and a higher capacity computer which improved radar performance by allowing the tracking of one target while simultaneously searching for others. Threat warning, as well as electronic counter-countermeasures, also were improved over the initial version.

This 1978 photo shows the No. 1 F-15C over the Edwards Air Force Base desert. Interestingly, this plane carries what could well have been the first conformal fuel tanks. It is also loaded with both air-to-air and air-to-ground weapons, and was used in Dual Role Fighter studies, precursor to the F-15E. (McDonnell-Douglas Photo)

During the early 1980s, the time of F-15C/D production, a concept for an air cushion platform called the Alternate Aircraft Takeoff System (AATS) was considered. The AATS was a system which would permit tactical aircraft to take off from battle-damaged runways. The F-15, with landing gear down, would be placed on the platform and towed to the take-off area. With the AATS platform's engine blowing air into the rubber skirt, the F-15 could accelerate to take-off speed under its own power. Once the aircraft was airborne, drag chutes on the platform would deploy and separate the AATS for retrieval. The concept was never adopted. (USAF Photo)

MSIP F-15C/Ds

The Multi-Stage Improvement Program, which was accomplished between 1985 and 1989, resulted in F-15C/Ds with features giving them air superiority into the foreseeable future. Major improvements included:

- The structural capability to carry the AIM-120A AMRAAM, Advanced Medium Range Air-to-Air Missile. The AMRAAM is an all-weather weapon with its own radar seeker which provides the F-15 pilot with a launch-and-leave capability. This provides for true beyond visual range lethality.
- An improved central computer containing greater memory capacity, higher processing speeds and better reliability. This computer also allowed improvement growth for future systems.

This late-production F-15D is shown during a taxi prior to take-off at Luke Air Force Base. The aircraft belongs to the 405th TTW. Note that it is carrying all three external tanks indicating a long training mission is ahead. (USAF Photo)

The first flight of the F-15E was December 11, 1986 and this is the first production F-15E. The Number One honor is still carried on the nose. The LANTIRN system is in place with both a navigation (port side) which gives the pilot navigation cues in a wide field of view, infrared presentation on the headup display, which allows seeing in the dark. The targeting pod (near side) has a gimbled laser designator which can pinpoint laser guided air-to-ground weapons. (USAF Photo)

• Programmable Armament Control System which featured a multi-color cockpit display with menu and data transfer module allowing the pilot to "plug in" information from the briefing room into the plane's computer.

• Tactical Electronic Warfare Systems (TEWS). This system, which consists of updated jammers and threat warning receivers, can act to "mask" the F-15 from the enemy while improving the Eagle's threat detection capability.

The F-16XL was the competition for the Air Force's Dual Role Fighter and would compete against the F-15. Distinctive in its design with "cranked arrow" wings, this aircraft is a highly modified F-16 prototype. The aircraft could carry twice the payload, twice the distance of the standard F-16. Wing area is more than twice the standard F-16, and the fuselage was stretched almost five feet. The F-15E would evolve as the winner from this competition. (USAF Photo)

The vast complexity of the F-15E cockpit illustrated by the F-15E cockpit simulator at McDonnell-Douglas in St Louis. It's highlighted by the use of CRT displays where various types of information can be called up by the crew. The displays can be changed at will by the pilot or weapons systems officer (WSO) in the back seat. (USAF Photo)

Another view of the F-15E simulator at McDonnell-Douglas in St. Louis shows both cockpit locations. The cockpits are missionized and at the forefront of technology. They feature multi-purpose computer screens, a wide field-of-view head-up display, and up-front controls (i.e. nothing on the side of the pilot).

F-15E

By far the heaviest Eagle, the F-15E has a maximum gross takeoff weight of 81,000 pounds. Perhaps the ultimate F-15, the E version, as stated previously, has combat roles in both the air-to-air and air-to-surface arenas. The F-15E, sometimes called the Strike Eagle or Strike Fighter, is certainly substantially different from the earlier Eagles.

The F-15E actually had to compete for its existence, and won out in a fly-off over a highly-modified F-16, called the F-16XL, in an evaluation known as the Dual Role Fighter (DRF) program.

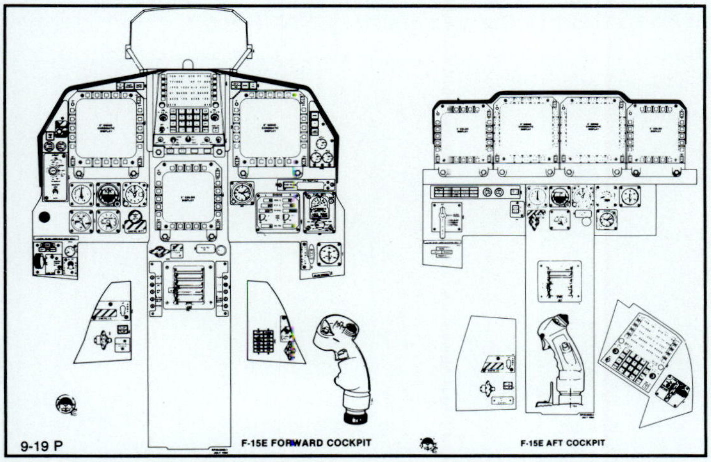

This McDonnell-Douglas drawing shows the F-15E front and rear cockpit layouts. Comparing this layout with the F-15A/B shows the almost-complete-removal of instrumentation on both sides of the pilot. Also, the forward cockpit features a side mounted control stick. (McDonnell-Douglas Drawing)

This particular F-15C, the first production model, which was used for research and development on the F-15E, tested the concept of conformal fuel tanks. Note that weapons stations are located on the tanks themselves, in this case carrying a pair of AIM-7 air defense missiles. (McDonnell-Douglas Photo)

Four F-15 models were used in the DRF flight test program. F-15D #27 was used for weapons separation tests and flew 22 sorties. F-15B #2 was used for evaluating the synthetic aperture radar which made 67 sorties logging 122.2 hours. F-15C #1 was used for conducting fully-instrumented performance and flight quantities evaluation and carried conformal fuel tanks and accomplished 91 sorties. F-15D #36 was the aircraft which technicians used for operational evaluation which flew 36 sorties.

The Air Force announced its choice of the F-15 for its Dual Role Fighter in February 1984.

The emphasis, as far as the Eagle manufacturer was concerned, was toward a two-seat configuration. Two crew members simply were necessary to operate the complex avionics required for day or night, all-weather operations especially against air-to-surface targets.

As one might expect, the complexity – plus emerging presentation capabilities – eventually resulted in providing the F-15E with the most advanced cockpit in the fighter inventory.

The front cockpit features three cathode ray tube (CRT) multi-function displays, while the rear cockpit gives the Weapon System Officer four CRT displays to provide navigation, target, and weapon information. The pilot's cockpit also features a wide field-of-view Heads-Up display (HUD) for use with the LANTIRN (Low Altitude Navigation and Targeting Infrared System for Night) system.

This operational F-15E, from the 4th TFW at Seymour Johnson Air Force Base, is in full afterburner and carrying external fuel tanks. This unit was extremely effective during Desert Storm. (McDonnell-Douglas Photo)

The two cockpit displays allow both the pilot and "wizzo" to simultaneously monitor the aircraft, sensors, weapons status, and threat defenses.

Giving an air superiority fighter the ability to accurately attack surface targets required significant technology evolution. One of those evolved systems is LANTIRN.

Built by Martin Marietta, LANTIRN physically consists of two pods. The Navigation Pod provides the pilot with navigation cues and a head-up, wide field-of-view forward looking infrared (FLIR) display. This is a television-like presentation of the terrain in front of the aircraft and is created by

The F-15E is poetry in motion from any angle. The prototype F-15E, tail Number 86-183 does its thing high above Edwards Air Force Base in the mid-1980s. (USAF Photo)

The first flight for the F-15E was December 11, 1986. That first plane is shown here in flight. The first operational delivery occurred on April 12, 1988 after initial testing was completed. The F-15E really did fulfill the Dual Role Fighter capabilities for which it was designed, both air-to-air and air-to-ground. (McDonnell-Douglas Photo)

Two early F-15Es are shown during a training mission in June 1989. These particular Eagles are attached to the 4th TFW at Seymour Johnson Air Force Base. (McDonnell-Douglas Photo)

With external fuel tanks, LANTIRN pods, two missionized cockpits, and the ability to carry both air-to-air and air-to-ground weapons, plus the conformal fuel tanks, these all contribute to the F-15E's maximum weight of 81,000 pounds. It's handled nicely, though, by the two Pratt & Whitney F100-PW-229 Increased Performance Engines. (McDonnell-Douglas Photo)

OPPOSITE: If you're an enemy bandit, and you find yourself looking at an F-15E from this vantage point, you are in serious trouble. Note the AIM-7's hanging off the corners of the conformal fuel tanks, and the extremely thin, low drag vertical tails. (USAF Photo)

differences in temperatures of various objects. The FLIR certainly "lights up" the night.

The second pod, the Targeting Pod, provides not only a narrow field-of-view FLIR picture for identifying targets at stand-off range, but also a laser designator stays focused on the designated target even after weapon launch allowing the pilot to turn and leave.

Other features of the F-15E include: the APG-70 radar with precision ground mapping, ring laser gyro inertial navigation system, a 3.5 million 16-bit word computer capacity, and integrated countermeasures.

The first F-15E made its initial flight on December 11, 1986 in St Louis. The second E flew in May of the following year. The second F-15E, like all succeeding E models, had features different from the original because of new manufacturing processes.

So-called super-plastic forming/diffusion bonding involves the heating of titanium sheets up to 1700 degrees Fahrenheit to make the material more ductile, and then forming it using high-pressure gas to blow it into dies of the required shapes.

Diffusion bonding involves fitting the formed pieces together under great pressure. This causes a binding to take place when titanium molecules

Kevin Hofele of the 4950th Test Wing, Wright Patterson AFB, prepares to machine a part for a dummy LANTIRN Navigation Pod for the F-15 program. The Air Force built the pods in-house for use in carriage tests at Eglin Air Force Base, Florida. (USAF Photo)

from one sheet travel to the other. This molecular intermingling produces greater strength than any other method. It's all accomplished in one single operation.

These techniques resulted in great simplification of support-ability and maintainability on the F-15E, since the number of separate titanium pieces dropped from 775 to fewer than 50. Another benefit was a 160-pound weight savings per aircraft.

From a pilot's point of view, the F-15E is a dream. Captain Greg Barlow, assigned to Nellis Air

Every new plane has to have a dedication, and here it was for the F-15E in December 1986. Here, both company and Air Force examine the cockpits of their magnificent new warrior. Note the size of the cockpits and canopy which really seem to dwarf the officials. (McDonnell-Douglas Photo)

McDonnell-Douglas certainly didn't hide its pride in being selected to build the first Dual Role Fighter, the F-15E. Here, jigs and tooling are in place for holding one of the thousands of pieces which will eventually evolve into an F-15E. (McDonnell-Douglas Photo)

F-15Es from Luke Air Force Base show off their maneuverability despite heavy loads of both air-to-air and air-to-ground weapons. (USAF Photo)

Force Base, described the feelings and exhilaration of flying the Strike Eagle:

"The combination of air-to-surface and air-to-air capabilities allows the F-15E to fight its way into a target area, put bombs on a target, and fight its way to friendly territory without being tied to air escort protection.

"Avionics is where the F-15E stands alone in the F-15 family. When you climb into either cockpit, the first thing that catches your eye is the lack of numerous 'round dials', switches, and gauges that dominate the F-15A-D cockpits. Basic standby gauges and essential cockpit control panels are present but the Strike Eagle cockpit avionics revolve around the Multi-Purpose Displays (MPDs).

"The front cockpit houses two monochromatic displays and one Multi-Purpose Color Display (MPCD). The rear cockpit has two monochrome and two color displays. These displays control nearly all of the aircraft avionics to include radar, navigation equipment, LANTIRN, armament, and several other critical avionic units.

"Once the jet is up and running, aircrews simply select the radar, via the MPD push button, to be displayed on the desired cockpit MPD. In this manner, the cockpit can literally be customized by each individual aircrew as desired for mission execution. Display choices are not merely limited to one display per MPD. Aircrews can program up to three pages per MPD and them simply scroll through the display via hands-on throttle and stick to view or control the desired display.

"The Strike Eagle radar is the same as that used by the F-15C. The APG-70 radar is argu-

The F-15E has been a huge recipient of wind tunnel testing, both at McDonnell-Douglas and USAF's Arnold Engineering Development Center. Store separation testing using five percent scale models began in 1985. In all, more than 500 aircraft/store configurations have been investigated to ensure that the F-15E can safely deliver the wide array of weapons needed to accomplish its air-to-ground and air-to-air missions. (USAF Photo)

This AEDC testing evaluated F-15E engine performance during the simulated low level, high speed portion of the fighter's flight envelope. During this 1992 testing, the engine underwent the pressure and thermal cycles that it would likely face during a combat mission. (USAF Photo)

ably the best radar set currently flown by any fighter in the world.

"Putting bombs on target is a difficult enough task that becomes increasingly complicated when the bad guys are intent on shooting you down with their fighters rather than letting you simply bomb their home base. Therefore, the Strike Eagle radar retains the same air-to-air capability of the F-15C allowing the aircrew to dispose of enemy aircraft as necessary on target ingress or egress.

"But radar isn't merely an air-to-air asset. Little do most single-seat Eagle drivers realize, but the APG-70 air-to-ground target mapping capability is second to none. Utilizing synthetic aperture radar techniques, the Strike Eagle can radar map and designate a target with near photographic resolution. Air-to-ground radar combined with LANTIRN targeting pod capability creates a deadly combination in the arena of air-to-ground weapons employment.

"As for other flying qualities of the Strike Eagle, the basics are relatively easy. When learning to fly the jet, you find that everything flows smoothly. Aerobatics, formation flying, and navigational tasks are easily learned. The avionics take a few sorties to get used to, but most pilots achieve basic qualification in four-to-six sorties.

"The aircraft is fully instrumented for all manner of instrument approaches, and future software enhancements will allow the crew to fly precision lights-out approaches with onboard sensors alone. That, in itself, attests to the future of the Strike Eagle."

Engines

All F-15s are powered by Pratt & Whitney engines. F-15A/Bs and C/Ds carried F100-PW-100 engines. Nearly identical engines, designated F100-PW-200, were installed in early F-16s and some early F-15C/Ds.

With the introduction of MSIP F-15C/Ds, the engine type selected was Pratt & Whitney's entry into what was known informally as the "Great Engine War," and formally as the Alternate Fighter Engine Competition. This competition was with General Electric for the fighter engine business. The Air Force-conducted competition was an effort to get higher engine reliability, greater warranty, and with the same maximum thrust rating of approximately 25,000 pounds. GE's entry was designated the F110-GE-100 and Pratt & Whitney's was the F100-PW-220.

The follow-on to the six-year AFE competition was the IPE (Increased Performance Engine) competition. The Air Force wanted increased thrust (approximately 29,000 pounds) with the same sort of reliability as designed to use IPE's from either engine contractor, the Pratt & Whitney F100-PW-229 powers F-15Es. The additional thrust maintains classic Eagle Mach 2.5 plus capabilities despite the additional airframe weight.

Chapter IV
FOREIGN EAGLES

Like many other USAF fighters of the past, the F-15 was immediately coveted by a number of other nations. Of course, the contractor would love to sell as many as possible in order to keep the production lines humming for years. But politics always seem to play heavily in these decisions as there are certain countries that were not deemed acceptable to receive the advanced fighter.

Also, the cost of the plane – considerably more than the single F100-engined F-16 – made that fighter more attractive to many countries.

Interestingly, the Shah of Iran was the first to show interest in the Eagle. It came down to a tough choice between the Grumman F-14 Tomcat and the F-15. The decision was made to go with the F-14 because its development program was further along at the time. Those planes would later be used in the war with Iraq.

The German Air Force also evaluated a possible F-15 purchase in 1975, but the decision was made not to buy. The Eagle was also demonstrated to Canada that same year. The Canadians would later purchase the F-18.

A month later, the British looked over the Eagle, followed by the French. Internal pressure, though, to purchase native-built aircraft probably played heavily on the failure of both countries to purchase the F-15.

Four Israeli F-15s fly over the ancient ruins of Masada, which is a symbol to Israeli resistance to outside invaders. It dates back to Roman times. Note that the Israeli Eagles carry minimum external markings. (McDonnell-Douglas Photo)

The first McDonnell-Douglas assembled F-15J is shown in flight. Note the red circular insignia with a white outline which is carried on each wing and on each side of the fuselage under the engine inlet. (McDonnell-Douglas Photo)

You can certainly bet that, with the success the F-15 has demonstrated to date, that a number of those countries might have second thoughts on not buying the plane. But with the continued production of the Eagle with the Saudi's making an additional purchase in the early 1990s, the Eagle could reappear as a viable export fighter aircraft.

But when all the negotiations to date were over, three countries received the Eagle: Japan, Israel and Saudi Arabia. The latter two have used their Eagles in combat. Following are the facts and figures on the use of the Eagle for each of these countries.

JAPAN (PEACE EAGLE)

During the mid-1970s, the Japan Air Defense Force began looking for a fighter to work with its Phantom II fleet. The new fighter was needed to fulfil the air defense mission. The Japanese looked at a number of both American and foreign entries before narrowing the list down to three American fighters-the F-14 and F-16, besides the obvious F-15.

For various reasons, the F-16 and F-14 aircraft were ruled out in favor of the Eagle. In 1978, the Mitsubishi Company was selected as the prime contractor to accomplish much of the production. The designations for the versions were F-15J for

On 15 July 1980, the first F-15J was accepted by the JASDF in St Louis. This aircraft would be flight tested later at Gifu Air Base in Japan. (McDonnell-Douglas Photo)

These patches indicate the organizational subordination of the first F-15J unit. The 202 patch indicates the 202 Hikotai (squadron) and the 5th Tactical Wing patch indicates the 5 Kokudan (wing). (McDonnell-Douglas Photo)

The second (and final) McDonnell-Douglas production F-15J is shown in flight carrying the centerline external fuel tank. The two Js were joined by a dozen F-15DJ two-seaters, all produced at the prime contractor. All subsequent aircraft were produced in Japan by Mitsubishi. (McDonnell-Douglas Photo)

the single-seat version and F-15DJ for the two-seat variation. The AIM-7E Sparrow and AIM-9L would be the prime weapons for the Japanese Eagles.

The first pair of F-15Js and dozen F-15DJs were manufactured by the McDonnell-Douglas prime contractor before Mitsubishi took over the prime production responsibilities.

The Japanese F-15s are very simply marked with the traditional solid red circle insignia on the forward fuselage under the engine intake. The particular squadron identification is carried high on the vertical fins while a three-digit number is blocked out on the nose.

An understanding of the Japanese serial number marking is required here because the system is entirely different from the technique employed in the West. In the five letter numbering, the first number indicates the year of delivery (i.e. 1982 would carry a 2 as the first number). The second number indicates the type of aircraft, in the case of the F-15, the number is 2.

Following the hyphen (-) in the serial number comes the mission type of the particular aircraft, in the case of the F-15, it's an 8 for the air superiority mission. The final three numbers are the identification for the particular aircraft.

Information concerning the operational deployment of the F-15 within the Japanese Air Self Defense Force (JASDF) structure is not readily available but it is known that the first F-15J entered

Four F-15s of the 202 Hikotai Squadron on patrol. The unique requirements of the Japanese self defense mission have been well fulfilled by the F-15. (McDonnell-Douglas Photo)

The second American-built F-15J, shown with maximum fuel capability, arrives in Japan following the ferry flight. (McDonnell-Douglas Photo)

Under the Peace Fox program, some 70 A-D F-15s were delivered to the Israeli Air Force. This A version carries a complete air defense ordnance package with both AIM-7 and AIM-9 missiles. Air defense is the prime mission of the F-15 with this air force. (McDonnell-Douglas Photo)

service with the Rinji F-15 Hikotai in December 1981. Other units were formed during the early 1980s to accept the new aircraft.

Like many other countries in the world, the Japanese military will also experience downturns in the 1990s. The leaner defense plan proposed for the 1991-1995 Mid-Term Defense Program showed a reduction in native-built military systems. Included in that reduction were 13 F-15s. Even so, the F-15 will undoubtedly remain the front-line defensive fighter for Japan well into the next century.

ISRAEL (PEACE FOX)

It comes as no surprise to learn that the Israeli Air Force (IAF) pushed the Eagle to its limit before accepting it as its front-line fighter. The IAF tested the response of the Eagle by making a maximum climb to 30,000 feet and a dash to Mach .9 in just over one and one-half minutes.

Some 70 Eagles now carry the six-pointed star of the IAF. The Eagle has paid for itself many times over with some 50 air-to-air kills without the loss of a single F-15! It's certainly a vivid testament to an

A very familiar sight on Israeli runways is the sight of an F-15 coming in for a landing. The Eagles are on constant alert poised to take off immediately if necessary. (McDonnell-Douglas Photo)

excellent aircraft manned by some of the best pilots in the world. As of the early 1990s, the IAF's Eagle inventory included about 25 F-15A/B versions and 55 C/D models.

As is well known, the IAF will modify fighter aircraft to meet its own operational requirements, and the F-15 was no exception to that rule. They were the first to use the conformal fuel tanks (built by Israeli Aircraft Industries) along with also starting the use of chaff and flare dispensers.

How the F-15s are deployed has always been kept secret. No. 133 Squadron, though, is known to have received the initial 25 A/B Eagles.

As far as external identification on the IAF Eagles, the planes carry a black Star of David (with a white background) just below the canopy. The unit insignia is then carried on the vertical fins.

As of early 1993, the Israeli's had decided that they would forego purchasing the AIM-120 for their F-15s. They did voice concern, though that the missile system was being sold to other mideast countries. Israeli officials indicated, however, that through honed tactics and upgrades to their existing Sparrows and Sidewinders, they would maintain their military edge.

Israeli F-15s also carry the native-built Python Missile, which is equipped with submunition warheads enabling an anti-Scud missile capability.

In early 1993, the IAF showed a renewed interest in the F-15, actually the export version of the F-15E – the same model which was approved for sale to Saudi Arabia. The Israeli Air Force had long been interested in acquiring more F-15s, but the aircraft's high cost (as compared to the F-16) and certain export restrictions had kept it from serious considerations.

On January 27, 1994, though Israeli Prime Minister Yitzhak Rabin endorsed the F-15 as the choice for procurement. Designated the F-15I, it is an Israeli-tailored version of the F-15E. The F-15I won the competition, purported to be worth $1.8 billion over a modified version of the Lockheed F-16. The Israeli's plan to manage an engine competition between the Pratt & Whitney F100-PW-229 and the General Electric F110-GE-129.

As of May 1994, few details of the planned purchase were available although some sources cite an order of 20 planes. Said to be similar to the Saudi version, the F-15I will feature avionics and subsystems uniquely tuned for the Israeli requirements for long range, precision attack at night and in inclement weather.

Believe it or not, this Israeli Eagle made it back. This aircraft lost its starboard wing in a mid-air collision. The F-15's rugged design and the fact the control surfaces still worked compensated for the missing wing, and the pilot was able fly the aircraft to a successful landing. This feat inspired a USAF study called the "Self-Repairing Flight Control System" which considered the use of a computer to compensate for damaged components in order to land or at least make it back to over friendly territory. (USAF Photo)

SAUDI ARABIA (PEACE SUN)

The foreign user of the most F-15s is Saudi Arabia who through the early 1990s operated 90 of C/D configured Eagles. A number of these F-15s saw action in Desert Storm.

The initial lot of F-15s carried -80 and -81 serial numbers. Forty-Six were F-15Cs and 16 were F-15Ds. Through late 1980s accounting, two of the F-15Cs (80-0099 and 80-0101) and one F-15D (80-0224) had crashed and were no longer in the inventory.

Then in 1992, 72 more Eagles-initially designated the F-15XL, and later the F-15S, (See Chapter III) were approved for sale to the Saudi's in a five billion dollar deal. The planes were essentially F-15E models (24 optimized for air-to-air and 48 for air-to-ground missiles). It was reported in early 1993 that the F-15Ss would carry the Pratt & Whitney F100 engine system after a heated battle with General Electric for the lucrative engine sale.

There reportedly would be changes in these Saudi versions in the weapons delivery systems, targeting, navigation and other systems. The Identification, Friend or Foe (IFF) System was also reportedly altered to prevent use against US-manufactured aircraft.

PEACE SUN PROGRAM SAUDI ARABIAN F-15C/D SERIAL NUMBER CONVERSION

F-15C	CUM	TAIL NO.
80-0062	1	601
80-0063	2	607
80-0064	3	506
80-0065	4	1302
80-0066	5	1303
80-0067	6	507
80-0068	7	509
80-0069	8	606
80-0070	9	503
80-0071	10	608
80-0072	11	1309
80-0073	12	605
80-0074	13	514
80-0075	14	1312
80-0076	15	1313
80-0077	16	1314
80-0078	17	501
80-0079	18	612
80-0080	19	1307
80-0081	20	504
80-0082	21	613
80-0083	22	1301
80-0084	23	1304
80-0085	24	508
80-0086	25	1305
80-0087	26	510
80-0088	27	614
80-0089	28	512
80-0090	29	604
80-0091	30	1311
80-0092	31	602
80-0093	32	515
80-0094	33	513
80-0095	34	603
80-0096	35	1306
80-0097	36	1310
80-0098	37	1315
80-0099*	38	1308*
80-0100	39	609
80-0101*	40	610*
80-0102	41	611
80-0103	42	502
80-0104	43	505
80-0105	44	511
80-0106	45	615
81-0002	46	1322

F-15D	CUM	TAIL NO.
80-0107	1	1316
80-0108	2	620
80-0109	3	518
80-0110	4	1320
80-0111	5	618
80-0112	6	1319
80-0113	7	1318
80-0114*	8	1317*
80-0115	9	616
80-0116	10	517
80-0117	11	619
80-0118	12	SI9
80-0119	13	520
80-0120	14	516
80-0121	15	617
81-0003	16	1321

* No longer in inventory (crashed)

The first Saudi F-15C is shown in the production process at McDonnell-Douglas in St. Louis. This was first C model of a total of 46, there were also 16 F-15Ds produced, all at St. Louis. (McDonnell-Douglas Photo)

The exterior detailing for the Saudi Eagles is considerably different from its USAF counterpart. "Royal Saudi Air Force" is blocked just aft of the nose with the same words in native tongue also in position just below. Both lines are done in a forest green-type coloring.

The RSAF rondelle is carried on the engine nacelle, different from the USAF Stars and Bars which is on the fuselage just in front of the engine intake. A small green RSAF insignia is also located on the outside of each vertical tail.

The Saudi's worked closely with USAF during Operation Desert Storm. The RSAF's two kills during that conflict came from a single F-15 downing two Iraqi Mirage F-1s on the same mission.

During the mideast conflict, the RSAF's Eagles interfaced closely with the coalition air effort. The Saudi's also provided aerial-refueling tankers, reconnaissance, and other support during the con-

Loaded up for an air defense mission, these Saudi Eagles carry a store of both Sparrow and Sidewinder missiles. The far aircraft (TN1306) was the 35th F-15 delivered in the initial lot known as Peace Sun. (McDonnell-Douglas Photo)

This Saudi F-15C was one of the first Eagles delivered and carries a different Royal Saudi Air Force designation, i.e. RSAF. Later versions would completely spell out the name in both English and Arabic. (McDonnell-Douglas Photo)

flict. The RSAF added British-built Tornados to its F-15s to materially aid the coalition effort.

During the 1990s, the Saudi Air Force is also looking to augment their ever-growing F-15 fleet with the possible purchase of additional Tornados. There is also consideration to purchase either the F-16 or F/A-18s to replace the RSAF's aging F-5 fleet.

Note that the Saudi F-15s carried conformal fuel tanks the front portion of which carries the forest green Saudi insignia. Insignias are carried on the wings and a unit insignia on the vertical tails. (McDonnell-Douglas Photo)

Chapter V
COMBAT

The proof, of course, of an aircraft comes when it's put into the environment for this it was designed. The F-15 proved that it had what it took, no matter what air force identification is carried on its airframe. The F-15 continued to prove in the 1990s that it's still the best air superiority fighter in the world.

UNITS

The Eagle has been deployed in seventeen different USAF units in the United States, Alaska, Germany, United Kingdom, Japan, and Iceland. The deployment includes all produced models (A-E) of the aircraft.

These F-15Cs, from Luke Air Force Base, really pour on the coal in a vertical climb at some 80 degrees of attitude somewhere over Arizona. (McDonnell-Douglas Photo)

This F-15A, of the 36th Fighter Wing was one of the first to be deployed to Europe. It has been reported that the 36th will be disbanded with its aircraft dispersed to other units. (USAF Photo)

The 555th Tactical Fighter Training Squadron received the first Eagle, a 1973-built TF-15A (73-108). The equipping was considered to be so significant that then-President Ford was present for the ceremony.

It wouldn't be until 1976, though, that the first F-15A would be assigned to an active unit, the 27th

F-15 Units (1994 Time Period)

Unit	Location	Command
3rd Wing	Elmendorf AFB, Alaska	PACAF
36th FW	Bitburg AB, Germany	USAFE*
33rd FW	Eglin AFB, Florida	ACC
1st FW	Langley AFB, Virginia	ACC
AF Iceland	NAS Keflavic, Iceland	ACC
405th TTF	Luke AFB, Arizona	ACC
58th FW	Luke AFB, Arizona	ACC**
48th FW	Lakenheath, UK	USAFE
20th FW	Upper Heyford, UK	USAFE
48th FIS	Langley AFB, Virginia	ACC
366th Wing	Mountain Home AFB, Idaho	ACC
USAFAWC	Eglin AFB, Florida	ACC
4th Wing	Seymour Johnson AFB	ACC
325th FW	Tyndall AFB, Florida	ACC
57th FW	Nellis AFB, Nevada	ACC
18th Wing	Kadena AB, Japan	PACAF
32nd FG	Soesterberg AB, Netherlands	USAFE***
20th FG	RAF Upper Heyford, UK	USAFE
86th FW	Ramstein AB, Germany	USAFE
52nd FW	Spangdahlem, Germany	USAFE****
116th FG	Dobbins AFB, GA	ANG(ACC)
131st FW	St Louis, MO	ANG(ACC)
159th FG	NAS New Orleans, LA	ANG(ACC)
102nd FW	Otis ANGB, Mass	ANG(ACC)
142nd FG	Portland, Oregon	ANG(ACC)

* Deactivated in 1993 with aircraft dispersed
** Transferred to AETC in 1993
*** Deactivated in 1994
**** Acquired F-15Cs from 36th FW

This F-15E is from the 57th Fighter Group at Nellis Air Force Base. Clearly visible are the two LANTIRN pods, one Sidewinder missile, and the heavy-duty landing gear. Note the ordnance carriage stations on the conformal fuel tanks. (USAF Photo)

This beautifully-illuminated F-15C is stationed with the 1st Fighter Wing at Langley Air Force Base, Virginia, one of the oldest fighter bases in the country. Originally the headquarters for the Tactical Air Command, the base is now the location of the Air Combat Command (as of July 1992). (USAF Photo)

TFS of the 15th FW at Langley Air Force Base. The other two squadrons of the 27th, the 71st and 94th, would begin receiving their Eagles later in the same year.

Eagles next started arriving in Europe in 1977 at the 36th Fighter Wing in Bitburg, Germany. Aircrews flew the first 23 combat-ready Eagles from Langley Air Force Base to Germany in April of that year. The deployment would eventually involve the movement of 72 aircraft. In 1978, the 49th Fighter Wing at Holloman AFB, New Mexico replaced its F-4 Phantoms with factory-fresh Eagles. The first Eagle deployment to the Far East took place in 1978 when eighteen F-15s joined the Pacific Air Force's 18th Tactical Fighter Wing at Kadena AB, Okinawa.

This pair of F-15Es is at altitude over mountainous terrain in the western United States. (McDonnell-Douglas Photo)

These F-15Cs are attached to AF Iceland at NAS Keflavic, Iceland. Along with the F-15s stationed at Elmendorf AFB, Alaska, these Eagles are situated in the most northern climes of any USAF aircraft. (USAF Photo)

The TY tail designation of this Eagle indicates it belongs to the 325th Fighter Wing at Tyndall Air Force Base, Florida. (USAF Photo)

The venerable F-106 was the aircraft being replaced at four units-the 318th, 87th, 49th, and 5th FIS's at McCord, KI Sawyer, Griffis and Minot Air Force Bases, respectively. Later, the 101st FIS (at Otis Air National Guard Base) would receive the Minot Eagles.

Still later, the 123rd Air Guard unit would receive the 318th's Eagles. In another transition, the 57th FIS in Keflavik Air Base in Iceland traded its F-4Es for the second version of the F-15s, namely C and D versions.

In the early 1980s, the 43rd and 54th Tactical Fighter Squadrons at Elmendorf Air Force Base initially received F-15As and Bs, but would later receive C and D versions.

Five units of the Air Defense Command were equipped with F-15As starting in 1982. With the disbanding of that organization in 1988, the mission was then turned over to the Air National Guard which used both Eagles and F-16As at the time.

A number of other units received Eagles through the 1980s along with numerous other transfers being accomplished.

Although not an operational unit, the 57th Test Group at Nellis Air Force Base uses both early and E Model F-15s in conducting a wide range of testing and evaluation of new tactical combat concepts.

Below: One of the few Air National Guard units to receive the F-15, the 102nd Fighter Wing at Otis ANGB, Mass deploys this F-15A over Boston. (USAF Photo)

These F-15Es, from Seymour Johnson AFB and the Fourth Wing are not carrying the LANTIRN equipment as neither pod is visible. (McDonnell-Douglas Photo)

This formation of F-15Es are equipped with air-to-air missiles and air-to-ground bombs. From Luke AFB, Arizona, they are ready to demonstrate their dual-role capabilities. (McDonnell-Douglas Photo)

F-15s can be easily identified as to their home unit by the two-letter identification on the twin tails. The ANG units often carry the state identification on the tails with a color horizontal stripe across the top.

In the early 1990s, though, the control of the F-15 was changed radically with the formation of an entirely-new operational concept. The longstanding Tactical Air Command (TAC) ceased to exist with all operational F-15 units coming under jurisdiction of the new Air Combat Command (ACC). Tyndall AFB, Florida and Luke AFB, Arizona which provide F-15 flight training became a part of the new Air Force Training and Education Command (AFTEC). The reorganization was prompted by the required downsizing of the United States military. The ACC also placed all USAF combat aircraft under this one organization. The new organization aligned with the new unified US Strategic Command (USSTRAT COM), located at Offutt Air Force Base, Nebraska (former SAC Headquarters) which would be responsible for the alert force which included land-based ICBMs, Navy SSBMs, and manned spacecraft.

The F-15 was also a heavy player in a new early 1990s concept called the Composite wing, which the 366th Wing at Mountain Home AFB initiated in early 1993. The wing uses F-15Cs, F-15Es, F-16Cs, B-52Gs, and KC-135Rs which enable it to

This pair of F-15Cs comes from Soestererg AB in the Netherlands. This unit, which carries the CR tail designation was scheduled for deactivation in 1994. (McDonnell-Douglas Photo)

This F-15A, assigned to the 3rd Wing at Elmendorf AFB, Alaska, is shown being refueled by a KC-135 from the Tennessee Air National Guard obviously on some type of an exercise. Later, this unit would be re-equipped with the F-15E. (USAF Photo)

perform a multitude of missions including air superiority, air-to-ground attack, and heavy bombardment. The concept was tested in 1993 at Green Flag 93-3 at Nellis Air Force Base, Nevada.

Another experiment of the concept took place at Eielson Air Force Base, Alaska with the 343rd Wing and the Alaska National Guard 168th Air Refueling Squadron. The Wing flew F-16s, A-10s, and KC-135s to participate in a large-scale deployment of F-15s from Elmendorf AFB's 3rd Wing.

Left: This is what happens when training almost turned deadly. This F-15 from the Elmendorf AFB was the recipient of errant and friendly air-to-air missile. Fortunately, the pilot was able to bring it home even with the serious damage that was incurred. This is certainly a tribute to the ruggedness of the Eagle design. (USAF Photo)

All of the breed (F-15A-E) are shown in flight. Aircraft are from Eglin and Edwards Air Force Bases. Note the darker paint scheme of the F-15E in the lower right corner. (USAF Photo)

WILLIAM TELL

Fortunately, there's not always combat to prove whether a fighter aircraft is up to the task. One solid way the Air Force uses to verify the effectiveness of a plane is the so-called William Tell competition which pits fighter pilots and their planes against their contemporaries. It happens almost bi-annually at Tyndall Air Force Base, and proves who really are USAF's Top Guns.

The F-15 has been participating in William Tell since 1982 and has dominated over other USAF fighters and Canadian CF-18s. William Tell tests the pilots, crews and aircraft in a number of different aspects including the airborne employment phase, proficiency with the 20mm cannon, defense against a ground attack, and finally, a scramble and the clearing of a "hostile" airspace. On the ground, the proficiency of the ground crews is completely checked.

The F-15 became the winner the first time out in 1982 with the 18th TFW taking overall honors. The 33rd TFW took the overall trophy in 1984 with Captain Scott Turner, an F-15 pilot from the 32nd TFS, as the "Top Gun."

The 33rd TFS successfully defended its title in 1986, with the F-15 equipped 49th TFW from Holloman Air Force Base taking the honors in 1988. After a four year standdown, the competition was renewed in 1992 directly after Desert Storm with the 18th Wing from Kadena Air Base, and using F-15Cs, taking the top honors. The top gun was Captain Jeffery Prichard from the 18th. Guess it goes without saying, if you don't have an F-15 under you in William Tell, you can just forget it!

Captain Jeffery Prichard of the 18th Wing at Kadena Air Base, Japan was the TOP GUN winner at the 1992 William Tell. The F-15 wing at Kadena had top scores of the l2 categories in the competition. (USAF Photo by T/Sgt Dave McLeod)

WILLIAM TELL F-15 Results

1982: 18TFW (PACAF) was the overall winner
1984: 33TFW (TAC) was the overall winner
1986: 33TFW (TAC) was the overall winner
1988: 49TFW (TAC) was the overall winner
1990: Canceled due to Desert Storm
1992: 18WG (PACAF) was the overall winner

Besides William Tell, there have been since 1975 a number of "Red Flag" exercises which have been held at Nellis Air Force Base, Nevada. Pilots have indicated that this exercise is just about as close as you can get to real combat. Red Flag exercises in the early 1990s incorporated many lessons gleaned in Desert Storm. F-15s have long played a heavy role in this training operation.

Members of the 36th Fighter Wing from Bitburg, Germany carry an AIM-7 Sidewinder toward their F-15 during the 1992 William Tell competition. (USAF photo by T/Sgt Dave McLeod)

A common mission of F-15s stations at Keflavic, Iceland is the monitoring of Soviet bomber aircraft such as this Bear shown here. Both Eagles in this photo are C models. (McDonnell-Douglas Photo)

COMBAT

So those are the organization and training aspects of the F-15. Now it is time to examine the F-15's performance in combat situations, an environment that various Eagles have found themselves involved since 1981. Combat, though, wouldn't come for a USAF Eagle for another decade.

With an Israeli Eagle, a Soviet-built MiG-25 Foxbat felt the first Eagle wrath when it moved against an Israeli Phantom. Foxbat number two fell shortly thereafter to another Israeli F-15. Six Israeli F-15s also flew cap for six F-16s during the bombing of the now-famous Iraqi nuclear reactor.

In 1982, when the Israeli invasion of Lebanon was underway, F-15s ruled the skies and knocked down over 20 Syrian fighters.

The Saudi Air Force got into the act in 1984 when two of its F-15s downed a pair of Iranian F-4E

Two F-15s and an F-5 from Eglin Air Force Base participate in a combat exercise. (USAF Photo)

Two F-15Es from Seymour Johnson AFB, and a single F-15C from the 36th Fighter Wing in Bitburg are shown here during a combat mission during Desert Storm. (McDonnell-Douglas Photo)

Had the war continued, there was plenty of air-to-ground ordnance available for the F-15s to continue the fight. This is a storage area for a never-ending stream of bombs destined for Iraq. (USAF Photo)

Ground operations supporting the F-15 continued at a furious pace during Desert Storm. This was the first conflict that female ground personnel actively participated in flight-line operations in a combat zone. (USAF Photo)

Phantoms. These were strange circumstances indeed with two foreign countries – both flying American-built fighters – engaging each other with the good guys (at least in American eyes) coming out on top.

In 1990, Iraq invaded Kuwait and it was just a matter of time before the US would be involved. It came six months later with the Desert Storm operation with the involvement of some 145 USAF and 36 Saudi Eagles. The USAF birds came from the 1st Tactical Fighter Wing at Langley AFB, the 33rd Tactical Fighter Wing at Eglin AFB, and the 36th TFW from Bitburg, Germany. F-15Es came from the 4th TFW at Seymour-Johnson Air Force Base, North Carolina.

Twenty-four of the Eagles-E versions to be exact-were located at a new base constructed in central Saudi Arabia and called Al Kharn Air Base. 96 USAF C/D/E Eagles were stationed at Dhahran Royal Saudi Air Force Base, while 24 F-15Es were located in the United Arab Emirates. F-15C pilots actually accounted for the first 23 air combat victories, a number of which were the highly-advanced MiG-29s. It's certainly not surprising that one national news agency reported, "There's not much doubt who's the star of the show over there," pointing, of course, to the success of the Eagles.

Before going into the details of the combat scenario, let's look at the overall results as far as the F-15s were concerned. In all, Air Force fighters shot down a total of 36 Iraqi aircraft, with the amazing majority (34 to be exact) being accounted for by F-15s. Included in the F-15 bag were 31 fixed-wing aircraft and three helicopters.

Air refueling played a big part in F-15E operations during Desert Storm. Tankers, such as the KC-10s shown in the background, made it possible for 24 hour-a-day operations against the enemy. (USAF Photo)

Blowing sand didn't stop F-15s from carrying out their missions during Desert Storm, it just made things a little more difficult. It was necessary to accomplish a field fix on F-15 windshields which were being scratched by sand particles. (USAF Photo)

AIR-TO-AIR KILLS

The Pentagon has confirmed these Operation Desert Storm downings, as of April 12, 1991

Date	Unit	Aircraft	Type downed	Weapon used
Jan. 17	lstTFW	F-15C	MirageFl	AIM-7
Jan. 17	33ndTFW	F-15C	MiG-29	AIM-7
Jan. 17	33nd TFW	F-15C	2 Mirage Fls	AIM-7 (both)
Jan. 17	33rdTFW	F-15C	MiG-29	AIM-7
Jan. 17	33rd TFW	F-15C	MiG-29	AIM-7
Jan. 17	VFA-81[1]	F/A-18s	2 MiG-21s	AIM-9 (both)
Jan. 19	33rd TFW	F-15C	MiG-25	AIM-7
Jan. 19	33rd TFW	F-15C	MiG-25	AIM-7
Jan. 19	33rd TFW	F-15C	MiG-29	AIM-7
Jan. 19	33nd TFW	F-15C	MiG-29	ground
Jan. 19	36thTFW	F-15C	MirageFl	AIM-7
Jan. 19	36th TFW	F-15C	Mirage Fl	AIM-7
Jan. 24	Saudi AF	F-15C	2 Mirage Fls	AIM-9 (both)
Jan.26	33rd TFW	F-15C	MiG-23	AIM-7
Jan. 26	33rd TFW	F-15C	MiG-23	AIM-7
Jan. 26	33rd TFW	F-15C	MiG-23	AIM-7
Jan.27	36th TFW	F-15C	2 MiG-23s	AIM-9 (both)
Jan.27	36th TFW	F-15C	MiG-23	AIM-7
Jan. 27	36th TFW	F-15C	Mirage Fl	AIM-7
Jan.29	32nd TFG	F-15C	MiG-23	AIM-7
Jan. 29	33rd TFW	F-15C	MiG-23	AIM-7
Feb. 6	36th TFW	F-15C	2 Su-25s	AIM-9 (both)
Feb. 6	36th TFW	F-15C	2 MiG-21s	AIM-9 (both)
Feb. 6	926thTFG	A-10	observation copter'	gun
Feb. 6	VF-1[2]	F-14A	copter'[4]	AIM-9
Feb. 7	33rdTFW	F-15C	2 Su-7 /17s[3]	AIM-7 (both)
Feb. 7	33rd TFW	F-15C	2 Su-7 /17s[3]	AIM-7 (both)
Feb. 7	36th TFW	F-15C	copter'	AIM-7
Feb. 11	36th TFW	F-15C	copter'	AIM-7
Feb. 11	36th TFW	F-15C	copter'	AIM-7
Feb. 15	926thTFG	A-10	Mi-8 copter	gun
March 20	36th TFW	F-15C	Su-22	AIM-9
March 22	36th TFW	F-15C	Su-22	AIM-9

[1] *USS Saratoga* strike fighter squadron
[2] *USS Ranger* fighter squadron
[3] Su-7 and Su-17 are externally identical
[4] Type unknown

Source: Department of Defense

As documented earlier, one Saudi F-15 pilot had his day of days on January 24, 1991 when he nailed a pair of Iraqi Mirage F-1s, the only kills accomplished by the Saudi Air Force.

The 33rd and 36th TFWs were the top guns with 32 total kills between them. Surprisingly, there were no aces from those TFWs, but there was one pilot with three kills and two others bagged a pair each.

The 33rd was the top victory wing with 17 air-to-air kills-all of them fixed-wing aircraft. The first kill of the war came on January 19, 1991 when a 33rd Eagle downed a MiG-29. The 36th TFW scored with 12 fixed-wing aircraft and three helicopters.

Two other USAF units each notched a kill – the 32 TFW from Soesterberg Air Base, the Netherlands and the 1st TFW from Langley Air Force Base.

The Pentagon reported that AIM-7 Sparrow missiles were the weapon of choice with 25 kills, with the AIM-9 Sidewinder doing the job in 13 other occasions. Two enemy aircraft were destroyed by guns and another was actually chased into the ground by an F-15! The 58th TFS was issued the AIM-120 AMRAAM for evaluation during the conflict, but the new missile was never fired in combat.

A pair of Su-22 Fitters were the final two aircraft shot down, which took place during the cease fire period at the end of the confrontation. The Fitters were supporting Saddam Hussein's attacks on the Kurdish rebels.

But this was war, and no matter how effective the F-15s were, there were losses. They were very minimal to be sure in the Eagles' case, but two F-15s were lost to ground fire, while a third crashed on a training mission.

The F-15 demonstrated superb mission capabilities during Desert Storm. In mission capable rates, the F-15C/D demonstrated 93.7%, while the F-15E was tied with the A-10 for the best percentage at 95.5%.

In utilization rates, the F-15C/Ds showed a 43.3% capability, while the E was 38.7%. The average sortie duration of the C/D versions was 5.32 hours (the longest of any USAF aircraft) while the F-15E was considerably lower at 3.27 hours.

F-15Cs carried out the first sweep missions of the war hitting Baghdad. Then, F-15Es went on to accomplish their well-publicized "Scud Busting" mission.

F-15 pilots explained that the E version was well suited to the Scud mission with the LANTIRN navigation/targeting system and the APG-70 radar. That radar proved it had phenomenal range and resolution. Several pilots explained, "If the target had any metal in it, we could find it. You could tell from 30 miles away with this system whether a MiG-sized target had weapons or fuel tanks on it."

The LANTIRN system was extremely reliable and maintainable during Desert Storm. One F-15E pilot explained that out of 79 missions there were zero failures on both the navigation and target pods. "The enemy could run, but they sure couldn't hide from this system," another pilot explained.

F-15Es from the 4th TFW (the 335th and 336th TFS's) at Seymour Johnson AFB, North Carolina were given the tough job of attacking the menacing surface-to-surface Scud missiles in their ground

This F-15C was part of the build-up for Desert Storm, called Desert Shield. Equipment was being put into position some six months before the start of Desert Storm. (McDonnell-Douglas Photo)

sites. For the nighttime patrols against the Scuds, the F-15Es usually flew in groups of up to four aircraft over the suspected launch areas.

The 335th and 336th each flew more than 1100 missions with the 335th logging 4300 combat hours with the 336th acquiring an almost equal total of 3400 hours.

Weapons included the GBU-10 and GBU-12 laser-guided bombs, Mk 82 and Mk 84 bombs, Mk 20 Rockeyes, CBU-87 (Combined Effects Munition), General Cluster Bombs, CBU-52s, CBU-58s, and CBU-89s.

Developed by the Air Force during the 1980s, the Loral ALR-56C Radar Warning Receiver was carried by all F-15Es and by a large number of the F-15Cs. Other C versions carried the earlier ALR-56A.

The fixed missile sites were easy prey to the Eagles, but the mobile sites presented considerably more problems. Some ordnance was released by both F-15s and F-16s from as high as 20,000 feet to protect against enemy ground fire.

To address the mobile Scud problem, the Air Force devised a new operational tactic linking two previously-unused systems – The F-15E and the Joint STARS (Surveillance and Target Attack Radar System) aircraft. F-15Es were installed in airborne caps directly above the suspected Scud launch areas. The STARS aircraft then watched each area and when one voiced suspicions, they were able to divert the F-15Es onto the target.

That wondrous LANTIRN system, with its terrain-following radar, was so accurate that Eagle pilots were able to skim the countryside at low levels

The Big Three fighters of Desert Storm – the F-15, the A-10 and the F-16. (USAF Photo)

Captain Greg Barlow was a member of the 336th TFS from Seymour Johnson AFB and flew 40 combat sorties during Desert Storm in an F-15E. His recollections follow:

"On August 9, 1990, the 24 Strike Eagles from the 336th deployed to Oman, the first operational F-15E squadron to arrive.

Within 24 hours of landing, the squadron was standing ready alert for both defensive counter-air and interdiction tasking in the Persian Gulf and Iraq.

"The phrase, 'Train like you fight' has more significance in the fighter pilot's mind when you think of it as 'You fight like you train.'

"In mid-December, we deployed to Al Kharj Air Base, and were joined by the 335th TFS, our sister squadron and two squadrons of F-15Cs from Bitburg AB, Germany. Our F-15Es saw combat the first night of the war.

"Throughout the war, F-15Es were tasked with every conceivable, and some inconceivable, interdiction tasking. From deep strike Iraqi airfield interdiction, Scud missile patrol, and 'tank plinking', this plane did it everytime requiring bombs on target. Mission tasking was almost exclusively at night, at both low and high altitudes.

"Flying the F-15E in combat is an experience that has no comparison. After the adrenaline subsides, you realize just how capable this weapon system really is. It's quite rewarding to know that you've just taken the most sophisticated hunk of flying titanium and electronic gadgets up against a well-planned enemy defense system, survived numerous AAA and SAM launches, wreaked havoc on the series of targets, and most importantly, brought your planes home safely with no losses.

"Loaded with 11,000 pounds of bombs and a full fuel load, a full afterburner takeoff is the rule. There's a definite kick as the five stages of burner light and the acceleration begins.

"Even at max gross weight, the takeoff roll is short. Once out of burner, you aren't about to set any time-to-climb records, but you've got plenty of power to get up to cruise altitude and meet the tanker. Due to the heavy gross weight, topping off on the tanker usually required tapping min-to-mid burner on one engine to keep from falling off the boom. The complete refueling usually took from ten to fifteen minutes.

"Then, we'd get an AWACS update, confirm the attack plan, and assure that all systems were operating. Approaching enemy territory, it's lights out, spread to combat formation, and begin the combat ingress.

"The simplest attack option from low altitude was merely to fly level across the target and release the bombs. However, there were times that we'd fly up to medium altitude and then roll in on the target in a diving delivery, or increasing the stand off distance by lofting the weapons from a low altitude, or employ a combination of these attacks to release laser guided bombs.

"Once the weapons were released, the primary concern was getting away from the target area. Bombs going off have an unnatural ability to start the AAA gunners firing. For the most part, by the time someone knows they're being attacked, you're already off target going in the opposite direction.

"Low altitude employment wasn't the only place the F-15E was employed successfully. In fact, when target, threat, and weather circumstance required, the Strike Eagle was equally effective at medium altitudes."

on Scud runs. The low-level capability made them almost immune to ground fire and Iraqi radar.

Post-DESERT STORM

But even after the termination of Desert Storm, Sadaam Hussein was still in place and making threats in early 1993. It would be up to the F-15 to come into play again and help quiet things down. Ten F-15s would participate in raids along with six F-117s, four F-16s, eight Navy A-6s, six F/A-18s, and six French Mirages. The goal of the initial mission was to blast surface-to-air missile sites located in the so-called "no-fly" zones. The HARM missile was effectively used by the F-15s in the attack.

Three F-15s, flanked by a pair of F-16s, fly over oil well fires in Kuwait. This was one of the most famous photos of the war. The Syracuse ANG F-16 in the foreground was part of the first Air National Guard unit to go to Desert Storm. (USAF Photo)

This 1st Fighter Wing F-15 was parked at the entrance of one of the Saudi-built aircraft bunkers. USAF aircraft were never attacked on the ground, but it was still nice to have them. (USAF Photo)

A pair of F-15Cs on an air-to-air combat mission during Desert Storm. These Eagles are carrying Sidewinders and the three external fuel tanks. (USAF Photo)

In a second raid shortly thereafter, an F-15 accomplished a probable aircraft kill. Though unconfirmed, there was substantial evidence that the victim was an Iraqi MiG-25 Foxbat. There were be more confrontations in the months to come.

F-15 pilots experienced only token anti-aircraft ground fire during these operations. The targets included Tallil and Samawah. The ordnance carried depended on whether the targets were command and control facilities or surface to air missile sites. Each F-15 was given one specific target to engage in this post-war activity.

Then, during the summer of 1993, action took place again in the No-Fire zone with F-15s again being involved. The event took place when USAF fighters reacted to Iraqi surface-to-air missile launcher activity. Two F-15s were involved with a pair of Eagles releasing four laser-guided bombs.

It wouldn't long before F-15s would be put in the line of fire again, this time early in 1993 in a different location when F-15s began patrolling the no-fly zone over Bosnia-Herzegovina. Twelve F-15Cs from the 36th Tactical Fighter Wing at Bitburg AB, Germany, were joined in the mission by US Navy F-18 fighters along with French and Dutch aircraft.

A sad occurance took place with the F-15 on April 13, 1994 when two F-15Cs were involved in a tragic 'friendly fire' incident. The aircraft were on patrol over northern Iraq when their pilots apparently mistook two US Army UH-60L Blackhawk helicopters for Soviet-built Hinds used by Iraq.

Both F-15s fired, one an AMRAAM, the other a Sidewinder. All 26 people aboard the helicopters were killed.

The helicopters were carrying US, British, French and Turkish officers and Kurdish leaders from Zakho to Salahaddin, Iraq. They were in a 'no fly' zone established to protect Kurdish nationals from Iraqi air attack. Both helicopters apparently had their Identification Friend or Foe (IFF) systems turned off.

The Eagle would also play heavily in a major Air Force decision to allow females to pilot fighter aircraft. Lieutenant Jeanie Flynn was the first to benefit from the new rule, and shortly thereafter, she was accepted into F-15 training. She graduated from the training at Luke Air Force Base in 1994.

The F-15 would be a major player in that it would be the first front-line fighter with a female in its flight training program. Lieutenant Jeanne Flynn was accepted into F-15 training in the summer of 1993.

Chapter VI
MUTATIONS

Individual F-15s, like many other U.S. military aircraft, have in the past and continue to be utilized as testbeds or special purpose aircraft. There are several factors in selecting an aircraft for these purposes but they boil down to suitability and availability. Without a doubt, the F-15 has displayed suitability for several test applications and programs. Several of them follow here.

Streak Eagle (USAF)

One of the first special-purpose F-15s was the Streak Eagle. This F-15, the 19th pre-production aircraft, designated F-17, was modified in order to attempt to establish new time-to-climb records. The Streak Eagle was trimmed down to the limit with all unnecessary items – missiles, radar, cannon, tail hook, one generator, and utility hydraulic system, flap and speed brake actuators – were removed. Additionally, 40 pounds were saved by not painting the aircraft.

For the attempt, some specialized equipment was added, however. A restraint device replaced the standard tail hook; a noseboom with alpha and beta vanes to determine angle-of-attack and side-slip; and special battery packs and controls were added. Other special equipment included an over-the-shoulder camera, g-meter, standby attitude gyro, equipment for verifying altitude, and ballast.

The empty Streak Eagle weighed nearly 2,800 pounds less than a production F-15. Fuel varied from 3,000 to 6,000 pounds since only enough was carried to complete each profile.

The flights were made in early 1975, but as early as 1973 McDonnell-Douglas engineers were convinced that the aircraft could shatter time-to-climb records held by the F-4 and MiG-25. Altitudes and times of the records set were:

3,000 meters (9,843 feet) 27.57 seconds
6,000 meters (19,685 feet) 39.33 seconds
9,000 meters (29,685 feet) 48.86 seconds
12,000 meters (39,370 feet) 59.38 seconds
15,000 meters (49,212 feet) 77.02 seconds
20,000 meters (65,617 feet) 122.94 seconds
25,000 meters (82,021 feet) 161.02 seconds
30,000 meters (98,425 feet) 207.80 seconds

The Streak Eagle F-15, an F-15A which had all its normal accessories and equipment removed to be as light as possible, was about 2800 pounds lighter than a normal model. The bird was intended from the beginning to set new world time-to-climb records, which it did in 1973 with eight records ranging from three thousand to thirty thousand meters. (USAF Photo)

The F-15 HIDEC, standing for Highly Integrated Digital Electronic Control, was an F-15A test aircraft for carrying out flight research combining digital electronic flight and engine controls to maximize aircraft performance. This same airframe was also used to test and evaluate a self-repairing flight control system which detected malfunctioning flight control surfaces. The research accomplished by this aircraft could have applied to future military or civilian aircraft. (NASA Photo)

To put these feats in perspective: a Boeing 727 takes more than 15 minutes to achieve a 9,000 meter cruising altitude while the Streak Eagle did it in less than one minute! The Streak Eagle is now on display at the Air Force Museum at Wright-Patterson AFB, Ohio.

NASA F-15 Testbed Aircraft

NASA F-15 testbed aircraft have been used in a variety of tests – including joint tests with USAF. Some of the many tests performed are listed as follows:

- The Self-Repairing and Self-Diagnostic Flight Control Program grew out of an incident involved an Israeli F-15 which suffered a mid-air collision costing the Eagle its starboard wing. The pilot found that he could control the plane and made a safe landing.

The internal configuration of the F-15 STOL/MTD is shown by this cutaway. Of particular interest are the forward canards which are connected to the engine nacelles. Actually, these surfaces were F-18 tail surfaces. Also visible are the pair of two-dimensional engine nozzles. (McDonnell-Douglas Photo)

The concept of an aircraft being able to make allowances for changes and losses in its flight surfaces and controls was intriguing. If the pilot could land the aircraft or at least fly back to friendly skies, he could survive.

The F-15 testbed successfully demonstrated the ability of its flight control system to identify a component failure, isolate the failure, and reconfigure other control surfaces such as ailerons, rudders, elevators and flaps to continue the aircraft's mission or be landed safely.

A cockpit display was designed to inform the pilot of the control surface reconfiguration and show him what operational limitations must be observed such as reduced "g" loading, reduced angle-of-attack maneuvering, or reduced air speed and altitude margins.

• The Self-Diagnostic Flight Control System was an active program in the 1990s. The goal was a system capable of identifying failures in electrical, hydraulic, and mechanical systems in order to save technicians valuable fault detection time.

• The Highly Integrated Digital Electronic Control (HIDEC) program was a system (active in

The unpainted two-dimensional nozzle configuration of the F-15 STOL/MTD contrasts with the red, white and blue one-of-a-kind test Eagle. Clearly visible are the two lower thrust-directing louvers. There are also similar louvers on the top of the engines. (McDonnell-Douglas Photo)

This F-15 STOL/MTD would be modified in the early 1990s to the Advanced Control Technology for Integrated Vehicles (ACTIVE) configuration. This aircraft would incorporate axisymmetic nozzles which would provide even greater maneuverability. (McDonnell-Douglas Photo)

This two-dimensional exhaust nozzle is shown in testing at Pratt & Whitney in 1989. Two of these nozzles flew May 10, 1989 for the first time on the F-15 STOL/MTD test vehicle. Pound for pound, the exhaust system has the greatest impact on overall propulsion system thrust-to-weight capability. (USAF Photo)

the early 1990s) to investigate and demonstrate methods of maximizing aircraft performance. By means of a digital electronic flight control system, a digital electronic engine control, and onboard general purpose computer and an integrated architecture, all components can be made electronically to communicate with each other.

• The Advanced Digital Engine Control System, ADECS, was a system (active in the early 1990s) which integrated flight and engine control systems. It allowed the engine stall margin, or the amount of engine operating pressures which must be reduced to avoid a stall, to be monitored and adjusted continually. This monitoring allowed engine performance to be used that would otherwise be held in reserve to meet the stall margin requirement. This performance could take the form of increased thrust, reduced fuel

This photo shows the installation of the 2-D exhaust nozzles at McDonnell-Douglas at St. Louis. The 1988 modification took place on a 1971-built F-15B. (McDonnell-Douglas Photo)

Although not receiving as much attention as the 2-D nozzles, the forward canards – clearly visible here – are additional flight control elements added to the front portion of the F-15. Used in conjunction with the advanced nozzles, they aid in maneuverability of the aircraft. (McDonnell-Douglas Photo)

flow, or lower engine operating temperatures. Results included increases in engine thrust of 10.5% and up to 15% lower fuel flow at constant thrust.

• The Performance Seeking Control (PSC) effort was to optimize total aircraft engine performance during steady-state operation. Similar in aim to ADECS, the PSC was a longterm effort to improve the digital engine control system to reduce fuel usage at cruise conditions; maximizing thrust during accelerations and climbs; and extending engine life by reducing the fan turbine inlet temperature.

• The Limited Control Study related to the goal of the Self Repairing Flight Controls which included the demonstration of a landing of an F-15 using only engines for control. In the demonstration, the flight controls were deliberately locked

This specially-painted F-15B carries the names and symbols of the countries where the Eagle is based as of 1978. Note that the nose is painted in a Thunderbird-like paint style. (McDonnell-Douglas Photo)

and a computer-assisted engine control system enabled the safe landing. The F-15's cockpit panel was modified with thumb-wheel controls: one for pitch and the other for banking commands. The system was tied into the engine throttle commands. The system automatically programmed the engines to control the aircraft by varying the speed of the engines – either together or separately.This work was aimed at greater safety for commercial passenger carriers.

ICAAS

An Air Force Flight Dynamics Directorate program, begun in the late 1980s, was called ICAAS for Integrated Control and Avionics for Air Superiority. It emphasized Beyond Visual Range (BVR) multiple target attack capability, along with providing for closing tactics in air-to-air combat. The tools of the ICAAS study were computer functions which eased the pilot's workload in identifying and countering threats. The functions were: attack management, tactics, attack guidance, defensive assets manager and performance manager.

Attack management included the control of sensors, the provision of situation awareness and fire or weapons control.

Tactics was an aid to the pilot in assessing the combat situation and recommending and executing the most appropriate tactic. Attack guidance was aircraft trajectory control information to achieve an advantage over enemy aircraft. Defensive assets management was a function activated by a threat missile launch and corresponding options to defeat the missile.

Testing ICAAS included intensive baseline studies of simulations of the baseline – sans ICAAS – F-15 in the same mission scenarios. Full simulations of missions using a mix of current and projected threat aircraft to represent a mid-1990s environment were performed.

Planned future ICAAS testing would require two F-15B aircraft. One will incorporate ICAAS cockpit configurations and test functions. The second will be fitted with ICAAS computers. The two will have an inflight datalink to demonstrate cooperative functions.

Overall goal is the enhancement of fighter effectiveness and easing the pilot's workload. Tests were ongoing in the mid-1990s and results should begin to be determined by the end of the 1990s.

F-15 STOL/MTD and F-15 ACTIVE (USAF/NASA)

The F-15 Short TakeOff and Landing/Maneuvering Technology Demonstrator (STOL/MTD) was perhaps the most recognized F-15 testbed. Besides its distinctive white, red and blue paint scheme, this Eagle featured rectangular – "2-D" or two-dimensional, moveable exhaust nozzle.

The nozzles were capable of vectoring, or directing the engine thrustup or down 20 degrees, in order to greatly enhance maneuverability – especially when coupled with the fuselage-mounted canards which were additional flight control surfaces.

Another important capability was thrust-reversing. In this maneuver, the rectangular vanes could be closed to force the exhaust forward through louvers. This capability was demonstrated for greatly reducing landing length requirements in case of battle-damaged runways.

The STOL/MTD test program lasted from 1985 to 1991. It met most test objectives and successfully demonstrated the feasibility of using 2-D nozzles on future fighters.

An interesting follow-on program, begun in the early 1990s, was called ACTIVE, for Advanced Control Technology for Integrated Vehicles. This program used the STOL/MTD F-15, but fitted with axisymmetric vectoring nozzles for even greater maneuverability enhancement.

ASAT (USAF)

In the ASAT, or anti-satellite, program, the F-15 played the part of a missile-launching stage. McDonnell-Douglas modified an F-15C giving it the capability to carry and launch the 2,700 pound missile. The missile's first stage was from and AGM-69 Short Range Attack Missile, SRAM; its second stage from the 6,000 pound thrust Altair III Thiokol rocket motor. Other features included a seeker system and small rocket motors to keep the missile on course.

A live-fire test on September 13, 1985 involved flying the Eagle upward in a nearly vertical path to an altitude of 80,000 feet and launching the missile. The ASAT destroyed a U.S. Solwind P-78-1 Gamma Ray Spectrometer satellite used as the target. Despite its success, the test was never repeated and the ASAT system, developed to counter suspected Soviet "killer" satellites, was never fielded

The ASAT Eagle F-15 was a one-of-a-kind test aircraft which mounted an air-launched anti-satellite missile. The weapon was launched one time and a success was declared, however, the program would never move to operational status. (USAF Photo)

This F-15B, in April 1981, was part of the Integrated Flight Fire Control/Firefly III Program. The program involved the blending of flight controls, fire control, and weapon system technologies – together with the pilot's abilities – to enhance weapon delivery accuracy and survivability. Simply stated, the program attempted to enhance the pilot's capability to better deliver weapons during extreme combat maneuvering. (McDonnell-Douglas Photo)

Vista Sabre II

Future air battles will increasingly depend on more advanced aircraft capable of directing their weapons with greater accuracy and greater off-boresight angles. Helmet-mounted Tracker/Displays provide a ready and capable response to that threat and the Vista Sabre II program, which utilized a pair of F-15C testbed aircraft to test the concept during the early 1990s.

The program involved the equipping of a pair of operational F-15Cs for demonstrating the capabilities of this technology in air-to-air combat. The system was designed to provide the pilot with weapon status, targeting information, and other important, time critical, data necessary for effective air-to-air engagements at any head orientation without having to look into the cockpit or through the head-up display. Also a part of the test set-up was a Navy high off-boresight missile seeker with extended range capability to track targets at high angles off the aircraft's boresight.

There was no mistaking this Eagle from its unique tail logo which depicted an eagle attacking a red satellite. The mission was successfully demonstrated in 1986.

Below: This F-15B, modified for the Air Force Dual-Role fighter program, carried the name of F-15E Strike Eagle Demonstrator. This was one of four F-15s used in the competition with the F-16XL. (McDonnell-Douglas Photo)

This F-15A will never fly, but it's certainly an important one-of-a-kind aircraft. Mounted on a test pylon at Rome Air Development Center, Griffiss Air Force Base, New York, this early Eagle is undergoing electromagnetic testing. The plane carries a GBU-15 smart bomb under the right wing. A data link pod is mounted on the center pylon. (USAF Photo)

Many different types of advanced aerospace materials have been tested on F-15 airframes through the years. In 1985, two F-15 tail sections of composites and titanium demonstrated weight and cost advantages. Shown here, the forward wing root section of this F-15 is fabricated of aluminum lithium alloy in a 1990 test. (McDonnell-Douglas Photo)

MULTACK

Although not actually using real F-15s in a test environment, a recent Air Force Wright Laboratory series of tests using simulation system known as MULTACK.

Through development of specialized software, a realistic simulation of F-15E against Scud missiles which were searched out during the Desert Storm operation. The testing could add capabilities to the F-15Es to better accomplish this mission in some future engagement.

JSOW Testbed F-15E

During the 1994 time period, an F-15E was outfitted to carry the new Joint Stand Off Weapon (JSOW), the AGM-154 developed by Texas Instruments to carry warheads from 500-1000 pounds.

The new air-to-ground weapon is expected to be compatible with most current fighter systems, including NATO aircraft, which will allow foreign military participation in the production decision.

The test program took place at Eglin Air Force Base in Florida.

F-15E Glass Cockpit

Wright Laboratory at Wright Patterson Air Force Base was also looking (in the mid-1990s) into a glass cockpit concept for the F-15E using 200 square inches of viewing area, nearly double to standard F-15E.

The Panoramic Cockpit Control and Display System was developed by McDonnell-Douglas to tailor the F-15E cockpit configuration to meet mission needs, manage the mission more effectively, and increase awareness in the cockpit.

Such a configuration could find its way into a future fighter, or possibly a retrofit to the F-15E.

Below: Test F-15s at both Eglin and Edwards Air Force Bases carry a number of different modifications for specific missions. This particular Eglin F-15 carries a unique nose sensor for some type of weapons evaluation. (USAF Photo)

Chapter VII
FUTURE

In a world situation which is constantly changing, so too isthe way the future of the F-15 has flip-flopped. In one firm situation, though, the Eagle should remain in production until the mid-1990s or beyond spurred by the 72-plane order from the Saudi Arabians. After that, other foreign orders or possibly an order of modified F-15s for USAF could push production out much further. There is just no way to tell as the situation continued to be extremely fluid in the 1990s.

Is the F-15 the best fighter ever built? Many advocates of the Eagle would certainly agree with that estimation. In the early 1990s, the future of the aircraft continued to be debated in view of its performance in Desert Storm and the huge cost of the follow-on F-22. (McDonnell-Douglas Photo)

The F-4G Phantom has played an important role with its Wild Weasel version shown here. That role, however, will be changing as the F-15s will acquire that Enemy Air Defense (SEAD) mission. (US Air Force Photo)

The possibility of more powerful engines for the Eagle has continuously been considered in growth version proposals. Later versions of the F100 engines have demonstrated thrust capabilities of over 36,000 pounds. Studies have shown that such a powerplant (known as the PW IPE+) could significantly increase F-15 combat performance.

As is true with any high-performance aircraft in recent years, the contractor has also considered several large redesigns of the F-15 as an alternative to new fighter designs. The different company concepts were denoted with the names of F-15X and F-15XX. That latter version involved a larger wing and significant airfoil improvements.

A modified version of the F-15 was also considered for the so-called Multi-Role Fighter Program, but was not selected for that role although there were many that felt the Eagle could have performed the requirements.

One of those advocates for the F-15 was the commander of the new Air Combat Command, General Mike Loh who stated in early 1993 his preference of the F-15 over the F/A-18E/F version which was also being considered. "I can buy more F-15Es that are more supportable, have much better range and higher payload than the F-18," Loh explained.

Loh had earlier stated in December of 1992 that he felt production of the F-15E needed to be continued for USAF consumption. "I would like to continue to buy F-15Es because I don't have enough of the planes to do the mission that I'm currently committed to do with that particular aircraft." Loh also indicated that attrition and planes in the modification pipeline had cut the number of planes available for duty.

A later Rand study backed up General Loh's thinking which recommended the buying of two additional 72-aircraft wings of F-15Es. Whether that will occur remains to be seen.

There are many who feel that the cost of the new F-22 does not buy that much more than the still-very capable F-15. There has also been discussion for stretching out the production of the F-22 and continuing the building of the Eagle. As it stands in the 1990s, the F-22 would start replacing the F-15 at about the turn of the century with the total phaseout of the Eagle occurring in the 2020 time period.

As capable as the F-15 is, make no mistake, the F-22 is one formidable fighter incorporating many new technologies in the propulsion, avionics, flight dynamics, materials, and armament areas. It is truly the ultimate fighter from any aspect, but the huge cost of the system may cause reduced numbers to be purchased.

But even as talk of replacing the F-15 in the future continues, the Air Force continues to improve Eagles in the field.

One of the big efforts started in 1993 was to modify the F-15 to assume the Suppression of Enemy Air Defense (SEAD) mission that was previously handled by F-4Gs and F-16s. As a part of this program, some F-15s are being modified to carry the AGM-88 HARM missile.

Also, the Air Force plans to totally integrate and upgrade the F-15's Tactical Electronic Warfare Suite (TEWS). Currently, dangerous gaps exist in the plane's defensive coverage. 1993 plans called for outfitting the complete F-15E fleet before the same retrofit operation is carried out on the F-15Cs and Ds. The Air Force feels this added capability will be most effective in ground attack missions.

The gulf war was the motivation for some improvements in the LANTIRN system. The modifica-

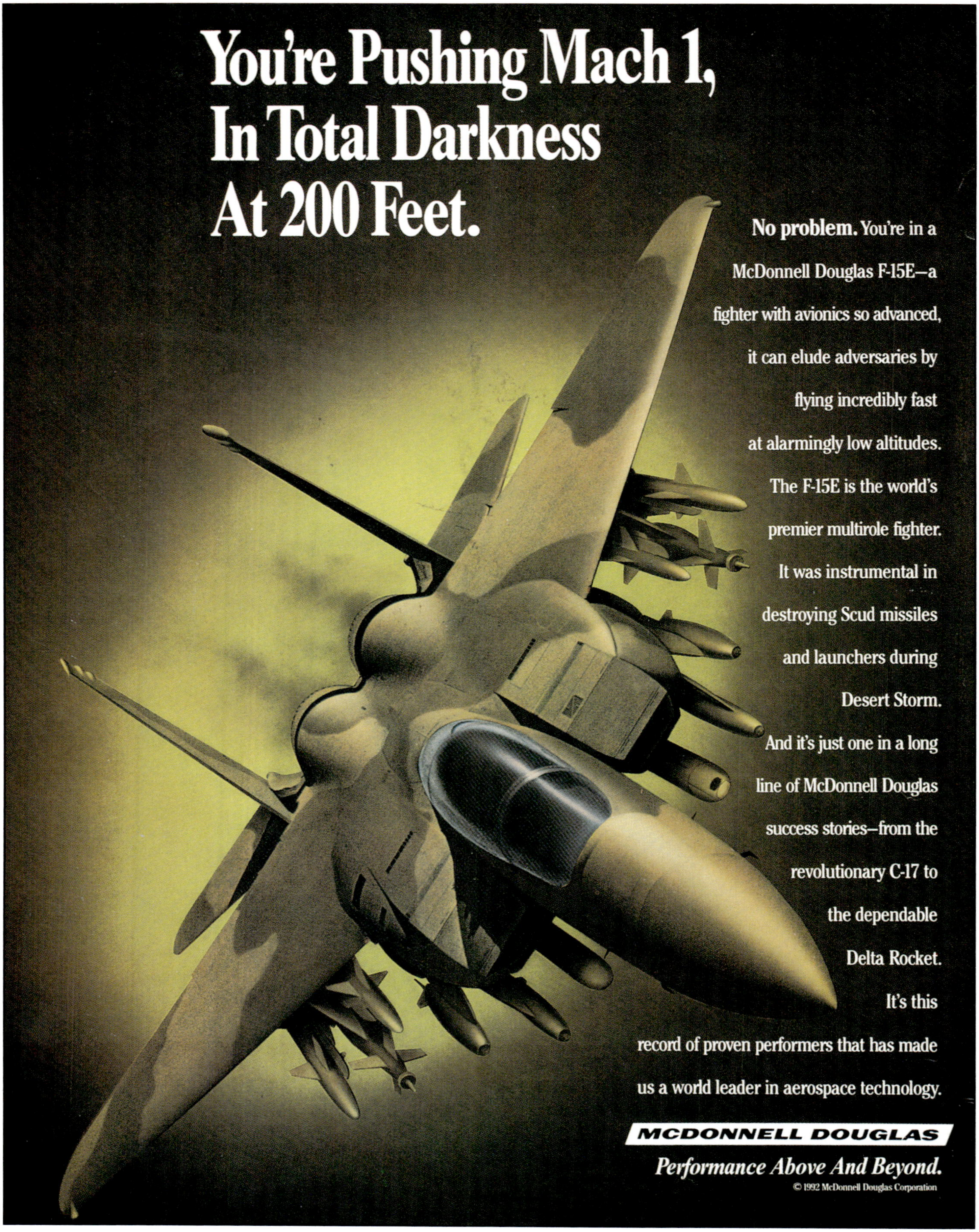
You're Pushing Mach 1,
In Total Darkness
At 200 Feet.
No problem. You're in a McDonnell Douglas F-15E—a fighter with avionics so advanced, it can elude adversaries by flying incredibly fast at alarmingly low altitudes. The F-15E is the world's premier multirole fighter. It was instrumental in destroying Scud missiles and launchers during Desert Storm. And it's just one in a long line of McDonnell Douglas success stories—from the revolutionary C-17 to the dependable Delta Rocket. It's this record of proven performers that has made us a world leader in aerospace technology.
MCDONNELL DOUGLAS
Performance Above And Beyond.
© 1992 McDonnell Douglas Corporation

An early artist's concept of the F-15 follow-on F-22. Note that there are similarities of this aircraft to the F-15 with the twin tails, although with the F-22, they are canted outward. There are also the twin-mounted intakes, but the F-22 has an overall more stealthy look about it. (US Air Force Photo)

A head-on view of the F-23, the losing contender for the ATF program. It is a great aircraft, to be sure, but it will really have to be great to replace the Eagle. (US Air Force Photo)

tions would provide for better LANTIRN operation above its performance ceiling of 25,000 feet. Since many times during the war, F-15s were pushed to altitudes of 40,000 feet and more, this change would greatly increase the capability of the already efficient LANTIRN. The F-15 System Project Office was also examining a number of other modifications in the early 1990 time period.

The F-15 fleet will also be the recipient of aircraft mounted sensors to warn pilots of attack by heat-seeking missiles. Planning for the 1996 budget has set aside $250 million to design and produce the sensors. There was some uncertainty, though, for the program in the early 1990s as there was the possibility that the program could be combined with a similar Navy program.

Research has also carried out on the F-15 to provide the aircraft with an anti-cruise missile capability. There is very little information on the program, called Have Yak.

And it goes on and on. Plans are also in the mill for retrofitting the F-15 fleet with computers utilizing Very-High-Speed Integrated Circuit (VHSIC) semiconductors. These high tech computers are expected to increase the F-15's processing power and speed tremendously. Maintenance will also be enhanced along with having significant growth potential.

It's interesting to note that the F-15 itself (in the form of the aforementioned F-15 STOL/MTD testbed aircraft) will also help determine the shape of future fighter aircraft.

No matter how current a fighter is, or how it continues to be improved or modified, eventually its time will come to be replaced. It will happen, even to the F-15.

Until then, the F-15 Eagle will continue to perform its frontline duties as probably the best fighter aircraft in the world!

Above and overleaf: The F-15's successor is the F-22, built by Lockheed, Boeing and Pratt & Whitney – it is going to be a tremendous fighter aircraft. The F-22 will use thrust-vectoring, a concept proved feasible on the F-15 STOL/MTD testbed. (USAF Photos)

OPPOSITE: In the early- to mid-1990s time period, the F-15 prime contractor was trying to convince the Air Force to continue production of the Eagle. There were even national magazine advertisements emphasizing its obvious attributes. This advertisement emphasizes the F-15's abilities at low-level, high-speed flight.

A FINAL LOOK

Unidentified F-15s appear to be stark black over a quiet ocean. (USAF Photo)

This "mystery" (and obviously inverted) F-15 test aircraft flies high over a western test range. (USAF Photo)

An F-15C (Bitburg) and a pair of F-15Es (Seymour-Johnson AFB) are flanked by a pair of F-16s over Saudia Arabia during Desert Storm. The closer F-16 belongs to the Syracuse Air National Guard, the first ANG unit to go to Desert Storm.

INDEX